A Century of
British Foreign Policy.

A Century of
British Foreign Policy.

BY

G. P. GOOCH, M.A.

AND

THE REV. CANON

J. H. B. MASTERMAN, M.A.

KENNIKAT PRESS
Port Washington, N. Y./London

A CENTURY OF BRITISH FOREIGN POLICY

First published in 1917
Reissued in 1971 by Kennikat Press
Library of Congress Catalog Card No: 70-118471
ISBN 0-8046-1220-X

Manufactured by Taylor Publishing Company   Dallas, Texas

PREFACE.

THE two essays contained in this volume were written at the suggestion of the Council for the Study of International Relations. It was felt that there was considerable need of a concise treatment of British Foreign Policy during the last century, and the Council wishes to acknowledge its indebtedness to Mr. G. P. Gooch and the Rev. Canon Masterman for supplying this need· It is to be hoped that the book will be found of value to all who desire to understand the development of British foreign relations. It should be pointed out that the Council for the Study of International Relations exists solely to encourage and assist the study of international relations from all points of view ; the books and pamphlets which it publishes or recommends are selected with that object alone in view, and the Council is not to be regarded as necessarily sharing the views set forth in them.

May, 1917.

CONTENTS.

British Foreign Policy in the Twentieth Century.

BRITISH FOREIGN POLICY IN THE NINETEENTH CENTURY.

DURING the first fourteen years of the nineteenth century, British foreign policy was dominated wholly by the great struggle with Napoleon ; and all the efforts of our statesmen were directed to building up, and holding together, a coalition strong enough to crush the French Emperor. In 1813 Russia, Prussia and Austria were induced to join with Great Britain in a supreme effort to end the long struggle (Treaty of Teplitz, September, 1813). The tremendous battle of Leipzig was fought in October, 1813, and at the beginning of the following year the allied armies entered France. At the Congress of Chatillon the allies offered Napoleon the boundaries of 1792, and when he met the offer with a temporizing reply, it was resolved at Chaumont (March 1, 1814) that his deposition must precede any peace with France. At the end of March the allies entered Paris, and in May Napoleon was exiled to Elba. The restoration of Louis XVIII. prepared the way for the First Treaty of Paris, by which France was accorded generous terms. At Vienna, in September, the representatives of the great Powers met to reconstruct the European system, which twenty years of war had left almost in ruins. With the Congress of Vienna, the history of the nineteenth century in Europe properly begins.

GENERAL PRINCIPLES.

During the century, British foreign affairs have been controlled, in the main, by five English statesmen—Canning, Palmerston, Gladstone, Disraeli, and Lord Salisbury. Up to about 1860, Imperial questions played a subordinate part in shaping our foreign policy ; after

that time our relations with other Powers were affected
less by European than by extra-European questions, and
our policy, in regard to all strictly European matters,
was one of non-intervention, except in Eastern Europe,
where the control of the Eastern Mediterranean seemed
to involve the security of our connexion with our Indian
Empire.

Throughout the whole period three general principles
gave continuity to our foreign policy.

1. Hostility with France had been the most permanent
characteristic of British policy during the whole of the
eighteenth century (1688-1815) ;   co-operation with
France was an equally marked tendency during the
whole of the nineteenth century.   The degree of
cordiality of this *entente* varied greatly from time to
time, and on at least three occasions, the two nations
were within measurable distance of open hostility ;
but common interests and sympathies enabled the
statesmen of the two countries to work together in
regard to most European questions.

2. The maintenance of the Ottoman Empire was,
during the greater part of the century, the aim of
British policy.   As a great Moslem Power Great Britain
could not be indifferent to the fortunes of the
Khalif of the Mohammedan world, and the Ottoman
Empire seemed the only bulwark against the advance
of Russia to supremacy in the East.   As the smaller
nations of the Balkans gradually secured their independence, the Liberal Party in Great Britain became
less anxious to maintain the authority of the Sultan
over the subject peoples of his Empire, and before the
end of the century Germany had begun to supercede
Great Britain as the protector of the Turk.

3. The general tendency of British policy, especially
during the long period of Palmerston's influence, was

to support the smaller nations of Europe against the interference of the great autocratic Empires of Austria and Russia. Greece, Spain, Belgium, and Italy owed the maintenance of their independence largely to British help, and our failure to give effective expression to our sympathy with Poland and Denmark was due, in part, to causes beyond our control. In regard to the smaller nations of South-Eastern Europe our attitude has been affected by our distrust of Russia.

GREAT BRITAIN AND THE QUADRUPLE ALLIANCE (1814-30).

At the Congress of Vienna Great Britain was represented by Castlereagh, and subsequently, for a short time, by the Duke of Wellington. The fact that Great Britain had no territorial ambitions on the Continent enabled Castlereagh to exercise a moderating influence over the other Powers, but this influence might have been stronger if the British Cabinet had made up its mind more clearly as to its policy. When the inordinate demands of Russia and Prussia threatened to involve Europe in a fresh war, Castlereagh supported France and Austria in their resistance. On her own initiative Great Britain returned to France and Holland some of the colonies that she had taken in the war, and the British representatives secured a Declaration from all the Powers against the African slave trade. The return of Napoleon from Elba brought the Congress to an end in June, 1815, but before its final adjournment the four great Powers (with the addition of France in 1818) formed themselves into a permanent Committee for supervising the affairs of Europe. This Quadruple Alliance must be carefully distinguished from the Holy Alliance, which had no real existence except as a noble ideal in the mind of Alexander I. Of all the sovereigns who signed the declaration affirming their intention to govern their kingdoms on Christian principles, he himself and the King of Prussia were probably the only sincere believers. Castlereagh and Metternich were almost openly contemptuous, the former statesmen describing the whole project as " a piece of sublime mysticism and nonsense." High ideals were wasted on a Europe grown cynical through years of war.

While the Holy Alliance remained a " loud-sounding nothing," the Quadruple Alliance was a very effective reality. Under the leadership of Metternich, the Austrian Chancellor, it gradually became the champion of reaction, maintaining the peace of Europe by stifling the efforts of the peoples to secure constitutional reforms. Four Congresses were held in the period that followed— the first at Aix-la-Chapelle, in 1818, at which France was readmitted into the fellowship of nations ; the second and third at Troppau and Laibach, where the intervention of Austria to restore the Neapolitan autocracy was sanctioned ; and the last at Verona, in 1822, at which France was authorized to suppress the Liberal revolt in Spain.

The reactionary tendencies of the Alliance were regarded with increasing dissatisfaction by Great Britain. Castlereagh asserted that the Alliance had no right to interfere with the internal affairs of other States, but only to guard the integrity of existing Treaties ; and Great Britain formally dissociated herself from the action of the Congress of Laibach. Before the Congress of Verona met, Castlereagh had been succeeded as Foreign Minister by George Canning, a statesman of more definitely Liberal ideas, whom Metternich described as " the malevolent meteor hurled by an angry Providence upon Europe." In reply to the decisions of the Congress of Verona, Canning asserted that " England is under no obligation to interfere, or to assist in interfering, in the internal affairs of independent nations." When the French armies entered Spain, Canning replied by recognizing the revolted Spanish colonies (1825)—a step that gave occasion for his well-known assertion, in announcing his action to Parliament : " We have called a new world into existence to redress the balance of the old." A year later Canning defied the Alliance even more openly by sending a British force to Lisbon to protect the constitutional party in Portugal against the intrigues of the Powers.

Canning is also said to have suggested to President Monroe of the United States the declaration in which the " Monroe doctrine " (that intervention by European Powers in the affairs of the New World would not be tolerated) was first formulated. The action of Great Britain broke up the Concert of Europe, but it saved the peoples of Europe from being condemned to political stagnation by Metternich and his allies. The Greek War of Independence, which began in 1821, evoked warm sympathy in England and France, and after the death of Alexander I. (1825) Russia, under Nicholas I., linked herself with the Western Powers in supporting the Greek cause. In July, 1827, the three Powers signed the Treaty of London, by which they pledged themselves to secure the autonomy of Greece. A month later Canning died, and in October, at the battle of Navarino, the Turkish and Egyptian fleet were destroyed—an event that Canning's successors felt bound to refer to as " an untoward event " that they hoped would not disturb the harmonious relations between His Majesty's Government and the Sultan. In the Russo-Turkish War that followed, England resumed her traditional policy as the good friend of the Ottoman Empire, and it was distrust of Russia, quite as much as enthusiasm for the cause of Greece, that led the British Government to support the establishment of an independent kingdom of Greece, rather than a merely autonomous state within the Ottoman Empire.

THE FOREIGN POLICY OF LORD PALMERSTON (1830-52).

Several events happened in the year 1830 to modify British foreign policy. The death of George IV. brought to the throne a king of more Liberal opinions, and a Revolution in France established the constitutional monarchy of Louis Philippe, in place of the reactionary rule of Charles X. More important that either of these events was the rise to power of Lord Palmerston. Henry Temple, Viscount Palmerston, was born in 1784, and entered Parliament as member for Newtown in 1807. As an Irish peer he was able to sit in the House of Commons for an English constituency. After filling various minor offices, he entered Canning's Cabinet in 1827. A few months after Canning's death he resigned office, and spent the next two years largely in the study of foreign affairs, in regard to which he became the recognized exponent of the traditions of his late leader. In 1830 he became Foreign Secretary in Lord Grey's Whig ministry. From this time, with a few short intervals, Palmerston directed British foreign policy for twenty years with almost undisputed authority. His influence over the House of Commons, which after 1832 became more representative of popular feeling, was very great, and even the Queen had at a later period no small difficulty in retaining her constitutional right to be consulted on foreign affairs. His natural temperament was impulsive, sometimes to the verge of recklessness, but as the friend of oppressed nationalities he made the influence of Great Britain felt in many directions, and without involving the nation in war was

able to give effective support to the smaller nations of
Europe in their struggles for independence. His strong
belief that the power of England must be used to protect
liberal institutions and the rights of peoples sometimes
gave a " jingo " character to his policy, and caused
distrust and alarm in European diplomatic circles, but
it was seldom to merely selfish ends that his efforts
were directed.

The year 1830 was a year of revolutions in Europe.
Poland rose against Russia ; in Spain and Portugal a
long struggle began between the liberal and reactionary
parties ; and Belgium repudiated the union with
Holland that had been arranged by the Congress of
Vienna, chiefly through the influence of the British
representatives, who wished to build up a strong state
on the northern frontiers of France.

The Belgian question was one in which British interests were closely concerned. Russia and Prussia
were disposed to support the King of the Netherlands,
while France was tempted to use the opportunity to
secure Belgium for herself. But Talleyrand, who now
became French Ambassador in England, wisely recognized that the new French monarchy must not risk a
breach with England, and the Belgian question was, at
his suggestion, referred to a conference that was already
sitting in London to deal with the Greek question. At
this stage Palmerston assumed office as Foreign Secretary, and his influence was exercised on the side of
Belgian claims to independence. More than a year was
spent in settling the complicated questions involved in
the separation of the two kingdoms, and the friendly
relations between France and Great Britain were more
than once severely strained. The Belgian crown was
accepted by Prince Leopold of Saxe-Coburg, a near
relation of the British royal house, and when the King

of the Netherlands refused to accept the settlement, and evacuate Antwerp, Great Britain and France joined in armed intervention. Final agreement was not reached till 1839, in which year the representatives of the five great Powers signed the now famous Treaty of London, by which the neutrality of the Belgian kingdom was guaranteed.

While Great Britain and France were settling the Belgian question the other great Powers were fully occupied with the insurrection in Russian Poland, the success of which would have roused the spirit of revolt in the Polish Provinces of Austria and Prussia. The Polish Constitution had been guaranteed by the Congress of Vienna, but the Czar haughtily refused to allow any interference between himself and his revolted subjects, and the protests of Great Britain and France against its suppression were entirely fruitless. As any attempt at active intervention would probably have ranged Prussia and Austria on the side of Russia, the Western Powers were obliged to look on helplessly while the local independence of Poland was swept away.

In the affairs of Spain and Portugal, France and Great Britain found another opportunity for friendly co-operation. The ill-treatment of British and French subjects in Portugal by the absolutist government of Dom Miguel led to a naval demonstration by Great Britain in May, 1831, and another by France two months later. Soon after this, Pedro abdicated the throne of Brazil and came to Europe in order to vindicate by force his daughter's claims to the Portuguese crown. While declining to assist Pedro directly, Palmerston allowed him to enroll English volunteers for his expedition, and even permitted Capt. Napier and other naval officers to join Pedro's force. Napier's annihilation of Dom Miguel's navy off

Cape St. Vincent, in July, 1833, was followed by the loss by the Miguel party of most of Portugal. The death of Ferdinand VII. of Spain created a similar situation in that country. The succession was disputed between Don Carlos, brother of the late king, who was supported by the absolutist party, and Isabella, Ferdinand's infant daughter, whose claims were maintained by the liberals. Great Britain and France supported Isabella, and joined Pedro, the Regent of Portugal, and Maria Christina, the Regent of Spain, in a quadruple alliance against Dom Miguel and Don Carlos. The Portuguese pretender was soon disposed of, but the Carlist struggle went on for several years, neither Great Britain nor France being willing to allow the other to intervene effectively.

In the East the settlement of the Greek question left England free to resume her normal attitude of friendship with the Sultan. Palmerston declined to assent to the idea that the Ottoman Empire was a moribund institution, and profoundly distrusted Russian policy. Soon after his accession to office, new troubles arose through the claims of Mehemet Ali of Egypt to the cession of Syria as recompense for the help that his son Ibrahim had given to the Sultan in the struggle with the Greeks. Failing to secure satisfaction, Ibrahim marched into Syria, and carried his victorious campaign almost to the gates of Constantinople. Unfortunately, Great Britain and France were engaged in driving the Dutch out of Belgium, and were unable to spare a fleet to help Turkey. The Sultan was therefore obliged to accept an offer of assistance from Russia, and a Russian army landed on the shores of the Bosphorus. Thus checkmated, Mehemet Ali agreed to evacuate Asia Minor, and was granted Syria and Cilicia. As a reward for his assistance the Czar secured from the Sultan the Treaty of Unkiar Skelessi, by which Russia assumed something like a protectorate over the Ottoman Empire, one clause of the Treaty obliging Turkey to close the Dardanelles to the warships of all other nations in case of any war in which Russia was engaged. Great Britain and France protested against this Treaty, but Russia, secure in the support of Austria and Prussia, ignored the protest.

Warned by the events of 1832, the Sultan Mahmud employed the German general von Moltke, afterwards famous in Prussian history, to reorganize the Turkish army, but before this reorganization was complete, war broke out again in 1839 between Mehemet and the Ottoman Empire. Palmerston induced the five Powers to join in a note to the Porte and to Mehemet Ali, claiming that the question at issue must be settled by the European Powers, but Thiers, now Prime Minister in France, secretly supported Mehemet, who had culti-vated the friendship of France and employed French military and civil officials in the organization of Egypt. In 1840 Palmerston determined on decisive action, and secured the support of Russia and Austria for a policy of intervention. A combined British, Austrian, and Turkish fleet bombarded Beyrout, and captured Acre. Mehemet, recognizing the futility of further resistance, surrendered his claims to Syria, and France, bitterly mortified at the action of the British minister, was obliged to accept *les faits accomplis*.

Soon after this, Lord Melbourne's ministry was de-feated, and Lord Aberdeen, a cautious and unaggressive statesman, succeeded Palmerston as Foreign Minister. At about the same time Guizot succeeded Thiers in France, and for some years the two governments re-sumed the friendly relations that Thiers and Palmerston had nearly converted into open hostility. The Queen and Louis Philippe supported their ministers' efforts to remove misunderstandings, and in 1844 the French king paid a visit to England, and appealed for cordial cooperation between the two nations.

The most important service that Lord Aberdeen was able to render to the cause of international peace was the settlement of a long-standing boundary dispute with the United States by the Ashburton-Webster Treaty of 1842, and the subsequent negotiations on the Oregon question, which, after some rather violent language on both sides, ended in a sensible compromise in 1845.

In 1846 the defeat of Peel's ministry brought Palmerston back to the Foreign Office, the fears of the Queen being met by a pledge from Lord John Russell that he would exercise effective control over the policy of his impetuous colleague. Unfortunately, just before Lord Aberdeen left office, a new difficulty had arisen between France and Great Britain on the subject of the marriage of the young Queen of Spain. The rather complicated story is not worth telling in detail. The return of Palmerston to office at a delicate stage in the negotiations awakened the distrust of the French Government and led to what seemed a definite breach of faith on the part of Louis Philippe and Guizot. The *entente* between the two nations was broken, and two years later Palmerston watched without regret the revolution that drove the Orleans dynasty from the throne of France.

In 1847 Palmerston was able to win a decisive diplomatic victory in the Swiss *Sonderbund* affair. The *Sonderbund* was a league of the Catholic Cantons of Switzerland formed to resist the Federal decree banishing the Jesuits. France, Austria, and Prussia sympathized with the seceding Cantons, but Palmerston supported the Federal Government and kept the Powers busy with diplomatic negotiations while the federal forces suppressed the secession movement.

In 1848 all Europe was shaken by revolutions. Palmerston's undisguised sympathy with the popular movements in the Italian States and in Hungary brought him into disfavour at court, where the Queen and Prince Albert were strongly pro-Austrian. Undeterred by this, and by the remonstrances of his colleagues, he threw himself into the turmoil with whole-hearted vigour, offering advice to Austria, and almost open encouragement to the Italian revolutionary leaders. The established order in Europe proved too strong to be overturned, and the only success that Palmerston achieved was in the support that he gave to the Ottoman Government, in conjunction with France, in resisting a demand from Austria and Russia for the surrender of the Hungarian leaders who had taken refuge in Turkey. The British Ambassador at Constantinople at this time was a distinguished diplomatist, Stratford Canning (afterwards Lord Stratford de Redcliffe), who had taken a leading share in negotiating the Treaty of Belgrade between Russia and Turkey in 1812, and who returned to Constantinople in 1841, to become the guide, philosopher, and friend of the Sultan Abdul Mejid, and the practical ruler of the Turkish Empire. Under his influence important reforms were effected in Turkish administration, and he was thoroughly at one with Palmerston in the policy of counteracting every effort on the part of Russia to gain influence over Turkish internal affairs.

Palmerston's last important act as Foreign Secretary does not exhibit his statesmanship in a very favourable light. Certain British subjects had claims on the Greek Government for property damaged in various local disturbances in Athens and elsewhere. Of these claimants the most famous was Finlay the historian, a warm friend of Greece, and the most notorious a Gibraltar Jew, Don Pacifico, who set forth a preposterous claim for over £30,000. In January, 1850, the British Government suddenly presented an ultimatum to Greece, demanding payment of all these sums within twenty-four hours, and blockaded the Piraeus. The Greek Government met the attack with admirable self-control, and France and Russia interposed to prevent further trouble. The Greek Government ultimately paid a part of the sum demanded, but *Punch* expressed a very wide-spread feeling in asking why the British lion did not hit some one of his own size. Palmerston defended his action in the House of Commons in an eloquent speech, in which he claimed that every British citizen had the right to be protected by all the resources of the State—*Civis Romanus sum*—and secured a great Parliamentary triumph. But his conduct of foreign affairs was strongly disapproved of by the Queen, who complained that important steps in foreign policy were taken without her consent. A Memorandum drawn up by Prince Albert in 1850 expressed the constitutional rights of the Crown so clearly that it is worth quoting in full :—

" The Queen requires, first, that Lord Palmerston will distinctly state what he proposes in a given case, in order that the Queen may know as distinctly to what she is giving her royal sanction. Secondly, having once given her sanction to such a measure that it be not arbitrarily altered or modified by the minister. Such an act she must consider as failing in sincerity towards the Crown and justly to be visited by her constitutional right of dismissing that minister. She expects to be kept informed of what passes between him and foreign ministers before important decisions are taken based upon that intercourse ; to receive the foreign dispatches in good time ; and to have the drafts for her approval sent to her in sufficient time to make herself acquainted with their contents before they are sent off."

It will be noticed that no claim is made by the Crown to dictate foreign policy, but only to be fully informed of the policy that the responsible ministers of the Crown are pursuing.

Within a few months Palmerston again offended, by expressing to the French ambassador, without the sanction of the Cabinet, his official approval of the *coup d'Etat* by which Louis Napoleon made himself master of France in 1851. For this breach of constitutional decorum, he was dismissed by Lord John Russell, whose ministry only survived a few months the loss of its most conspicuous member.

THE CRIMEAN WAR AND THE CONGRESS OF PARIS (1852-59).

From the time when Palmerston took office, in 1830, the relations of Great Britain with Russia were generally unsatisfactory. The suppression of the Polish Constitution, the Treaty of Unkiar Skelessi, and the intervention of Russia in the affairs of Hungary in 1849, led a large section of English people to regard Russia as the bulwark of aggressive autocrary ; while Nicholas, on his side, regarded Palmerston as an instigator of revolution and disorder. In 1844, while Lord Aberdeen was Foreign Secretary, Nicholas paid a visit to England, and succeeded, for a time, in establishing better relations. He discussed the Eastern Question very freely with Lord Aberdeen. Believing that the Ottoman Empire was near its end, he suggested that a friendly understanding as to the future of the Sultan's dominions might obviate difficulties hereafter. While repudiating any ambition to acquire Constantinople, he said that he would not allow it to fall into the hands of any other great Power. The European Provinces of the Ottoman Empire might become autonomous states under Russian protection, and Great Britain might assure her route to Indian by occupying Egypt.

In 1852, after Lord Derby's brief ministry, Lord Aberdeen became Prime Minister, with Lord John Russell as Foreign Secretary (succeeded in a short time by Lord Clarendon). The European horizon seemed clear except for a small cloud in the East. Louis Napoleon had tried to propitiate the clerical party in France by reviving an ancient claim of the French to the custody of the Holy Places in Palestine, and had secured concessions from the Sultan to which the Czar, as head of the Russian Church, refused to assent. In 1852 Napoleon became Emperor of the French, having overturned the Republic by a *coup d'Etat*. The Czar marked his disapproval by addressing the new Emperor as "Mon cher ami" instead of "Monsieur mon frère"— an official discourtesy that Napoleon resented.

In January, 1853, the Czar, in view of the reopening of the Eastern Question, held three conferences with the British ambassador, Sir Hamilton Seymour, in which he practically repeated the suggestions that he had made to Lord Aberdeen nine years before. The only result was to awaken distrust in the minds of the British Cabinet.

In March the Czar sent Menschikoff, a rough soldier, to Constantinople, where he demanded from the Sultan, not only the concessions that had already been asked for by the Czar in regard to the Holy Places, but an actual protectorate over all Greek Christians in the Turkish Empire. Lord Stratford de Redcliffe, who had been at home for some time, was sent back to Constantinople, and acting on his advice, the Porte rejected this latter proposal, while offering to negotiate about the Holy Places. It was unfortunate that Lord Stratford was known to be on unfriendly terms with the Russian court,

and there is no doubt that he stiffened the resistance
of the Turkish Government to the Russian demands.
During the summer the two Powers drifted steadily
towards war, and in spite of Lord Aberdeen's efforts,
public opinion in England took a war-like direction.
As he wrote to Mr. Gladstone, " Step by step, the Turks
have drawn us into a position in which we are more or
less committed to their support." At the end of October,
war broke out between Russia and Turkey, and in
February, 1854, Great Britain and France withdrew
their ambassadors from St. Petersburg.

There is little doubt that the Crimean War might have
been avoided, at least as far as England was concerned,
if the negotiations of the year 1853 had been more
skilfully conducted. Unfortunately, the Cabinet was
divided into two sections, Lord Palmerston, who was
now Home Secretary, favouring such strong action as
might convince Russia, while there was still time, that
Great Britain meant to stand by Turkey, even at the
cost of war ; while Lord Aberdeen hoped to keep the
peace by a conciliatory policy. Not for the last time
Great Britain " put her money on the wrong horse "
(as Lord Salisbury said in 1895) by backing the Ottoman
Empire against Russia.

There is no need to tell in detail the story of the
Crimean War. The mismanagement of the war led to
the defeat of the ministry in January, 1855, and Lord
Palmerston became Prime Minister. The death of the
Czar in March, 1855, the fall of Sebastopol in September,
and the growing desire of the Emperor Napoleon for
peace, encouraged the offer of Austrian mediation, and so
led to the assembly of the Congress of Paris, at which
Lord Clarendon acted as British representative. His
task was rendered difficult by the marked friendliness
that the French plenipotentiaries showed towards Russia,

and in the end an inconclusive Treaty was arranged, of which the most important clauses were those that admitted Turkey to the public law and system of Europe, neutralized the Black Sea and closed the Dardanelles to all ships of war, and gave autonomy, under the guarantee of the Powers, to the Danubian Provinces and Serbia.

Before the Congress closed, some important changes in the laws of naval war were embodied in the Declaration of Paris.* In assenting to these Great Britain abandoned some of the claims for which she had contended in the Napoleonic Wars.

Naval matters connected with the war led to serious friction with the United States, and open rupture was only avoided by the careful restraint of the British ministry. Soon after this, Great Britain became involved in a war with China, in regard to which Palmerston's policy was condemned by a majority in the House of Commons, but approved by the constituencies, to which he appealed. The Indian Mutiny interrupted the Chinese War, which was resumed at the end of 1857, in co-operation with the French. A final settlement of the matters in dispute was not reached till 1860, when the Treaty of Pekin brought China, for the first time, into direct relation with the Western European Powers.

Strangely enough, it was not the aggressive character of his foreign policy, but his undue conciliatoriness to France, that led to the fall of Palmerston's ministry in 1858. An Italian named Orsini made an attempt on the life of the French Emperor, and the plot was known to have been hatched in London. An intemperate demand was therefore made by the French Foreign Minister

---

* By the Declaration of Paris (1) Privateering was made illegal (2) neutral flags were to cover enemy goods, except contraband of war (3) neutral goods were not liable to capture under enemy flag (4) blockades were to be effective.

that England should renounce the right of asylum that she gave to foreign exiles, and alter her law of conspiracy. Palmerston introduced a Bill making conspiracy to murder a felony, but the fact that it was proposed at what was practically the dictation of France ensured its rejection. To Lord Derby, who succeeded as Prime Minister, the French Foreign Minister explained away his dictatorial language, and friendly relations were resumed between the two Governments. Within a few months Napoleon, without the knowledge of the British Ministry, or even of his own, held a secret meeting with Cavour at Plombières, and agreed to join Sardinia in a war for the liberation of Italy " from the Alps to the Adriatic." When signs of impending war between France and Austria began to show themselves, the British Government laboured earnestly for peace, and its failure to avert the conflict led to its defeat in Parliament a few days after the French campaign had opened, Lord Malmesbury being supposed, quite unjustly, to have encouraged Austria in resisting a peaceable settlement. Lord Palmerston again became Prime Minister, with Lord John Russell as Foreign Secretary.

PALMERSTON AND RUSSELL (1859-65).

At the time when Palmerston resumed office, the British public were becoming profoundly distrustful of Napoleon III. The Volunteer Movement, which began during Lord Derby's ministry, found its chief stimulus in this distrust, and Tennyson, in one of his least successful poems (' Form, Riflemen, Form '), expressed a very general feeling in the somewhat unpoetical lines :—

> True that we have a faithful ally,
> But only the devil can tell what he means.

This feeling of distrust Palmerston now fully shared. Napoleon's demand for Savoy and Nice as the price of his services to the cause of Italy aroused in him a strong feeling of resentment, and he had come to believe, not on any adequate evidence, that at the bottom of Napoleon's heart " there rankles a deep and inextinguishable desire to humble and punish England." One of the first acts of the new ministry was to ask for a sum of £9,000,000 for the fortifying of the dockyard towns. The proposal nearly led to Gladstone's resignation of the office of Chancellor of the Exchequer— a threat that Palmerston met with the characteristic rejoinder that it was better to lose Gladstone than Portsmouth.

The years of Palmerston's last ministry were among the most momentous in European history. In 1859 and 1860 Cavour and Garibaldi, by almost superhuman dexterity and courage, brought Central and Southern Italy into union with the North, and set Victor Emmanuel on the throne of a united Italy, in which, however, Venetia and Rome were not yet included. The death of Cavour, at the moment of his triumph, left Bismarck the most conspicuous statesman in Europe, and transferred the storm-centre of Europe from Italy to Prussia. Palmerston's distrust of France and Russia led him to welcome the prospect of a strong Prussia, and British statesmanship placed no obstacles in the way of the realization of Bismarck's policy.

The influence of Earl Russell—though Lord Salisbury accused him of adopting " a sort of tariff of insolence " in his dealings with foreign Powers—and perhaps the mellowing effect of advancing years, now restrained Palmerston's impetuosity, and the influence of the Queen, earnestly supported by Prince Albert till his death in December, 1861, was used in the same direction.

Sympathy with Austria prevented the court from sharing the enthusiasm with which most of the British people watched the struggle of Italy for freedom, but Palmerston and his colleagues were able to give valuable support to the cause. When Garibaldi sailed for Sicily, Russell openly expressed the sympathy of the British ministry, and Palmerston refused to join in, or sanction, French intervention to save the kingdom of Naples. It was well understood by the Powers that England supported the claim of the Italians to settle their own affairs without interference from outside.*

The outbreak of the Civil War in the United States soon involved England in grave dangers. The arrest of two Confederate envoys on the British steamer, the Trent, brought Great Britain and the Federal Government within measurable distance of war. On the advice of Prince Albert, the Queen suggested a modification of the proposals of the ministry, which practically amounted to an ultimatum, and so afforded the President of the United States an opportunity of disavowing the act of the captain who had made the arrest. Palmerston and Russell were at one with a large section of the upper and commercial classes in England in sympathizing with the Southern States— an attitude that caused keen disappointment and resentment in the North, where it had been expected that a struggle for the abolition of slavery would have been able to count on the moral support of England. The action of the Government in allowing the Alabama to escape from Birkenhead as a Confederate privateer led to a controversy that was not finally settled till ten years later.

The year 1863 was chiefly occupied, as far as our Foreign Office was concerned, with the Schleswig-

* See Lord John Russell's dispatch of Oct. 27, 1860.

Holstein question. In 1849-50 the German Diet was involved in war with Denmark on the subject of these two Duchies, which, though subject to the Danish Crown, were German in race and sympathy (except Northern Schleswig). Great Britain and Russia had taken a leading share, in 1852, in settling the question of the succession in Denmark, and incidentally, the status of the Duchies. Just before his death, Frederick VII. of Denmark granted autonomy to Holstein, while virtually annexing Schleswig to Denmark. Christian IX., who succeeded, had to meet the consequences of this step. Into the rights and wrongs of the controversy, there is no need to enter. There can be no doubt that Bismarck recognized the opportunity afforded to Prussia of acting as the champion of German interests, and forcing Austria into a false position. Neither he, nor any other European statesman, saw clearly how the annexation of Holstein would, in after years, open a new way from the North Sea to the Baltic, and give to German naval power its strongest place of refuge. Palmerston was personally eager to go all lengths in defending Denmark against the attack of the two German Powers, but Napoleon, piqued by the refusal of the British Government in the previous year to back up by action a protest in which the two governments had joined against the way in which the Czar put down the Polish rising, declined to intervene except on terms that the British Government could not accept. It is doubtful whether British intervention would have done much to help the Danes, but it was unfortunate that Palmerston and Russell had led Denmark to suppose that it would be supported by England in resisting the demands of Bismarck. The Queen was strongly against intervention, and the general opinion of the country was with her. She even threatened to dissolve Parliament, if necessary, and appeal to the people against her own ministers. In the end, Denmark was left unsupported, but it is difficult to refute the statement made in a vote of censure, moved by Disraeli, and only defeated by the personal influence of Palmerston, that by failing to uphold the independence and integrity of Denmark the Government had "lowered the just influence of this country in the councils of Europe, and thereby diminished the securities for peace."

The Schleswig - Holstein problem was the last important question in British Foreign Policy with which Palmerston had to deal. In October, 1865, just after a general election had returned him to power with an increased majority, he died, within two days of completing his 81st year. With him closed the period during which England claimed the right of active intervention in all European questions. It cannot be said that Palmerston made Great Britain loved or trusted by the Chancelleries of Europe, but without involving the country in war (excepting the Crimean War, for which his responsibility was only subordinate) he compelled the other Powers of Europe to recognize that the opinion of Great Britain must be taken into account in all international questions that arose.

THE PERIOD OF NON-INTERVENTION (1865-75).

During the decade that followed the death of Palmerston, foreign affairs take a very subordinate place in English political life. Under the leadership of Gladstone, the Liberal party was occupied in carrying through reforms that had been postponed during the lifetime of Lord Palmerston, while the Tory party accepted Disraeli's view that England had "outgrown the European continent." "England is the metropolis of a great maritime empire extending to the boundaries of the furthest ocean.... She is as ready, and as willing even, to interfere as in the old days when the necessity of her position requires it....she is really more of an Asiatic than a European power."* In the spring of 1866, a conservative ministry came into office, with Lord Derby as Prime Minister, and Disraeli as Chancellor of the Exchequer and leader of the House of Commons. In the great struggle of this year between Austria and Prussia, Great Britain observed strict neutrality, but the efforts of Napoleon to obtain compensation for the aggrandizement of Prussia touched English interests too nearly to admit of the complete indifference of the British Government. A proposal of the French Emperor that France should annex Belgium only became known to the public in 1870, when Bismarck published the draft treaty submitted by Napoleon, with a view to alienating English sympathy from him. A demand by Napoleon for the withdrawal of the Prussian garrison from the fortress of Luxemburg was, at the suggestion of Lord Stanley, the British foreign secretary, submitted to a conference in London, and led to a " collective " guarantee of the neutrality of the little province—a guarantee that, as Lord Stanley explained, did not pledge England to intervention except in conjunction with the other Powers. At the end of the year 1868 the conservative ministry resigned, and Gladstone came into office as Prime Minister with a majority of more than a hundred. When the Franco-German war broke out, English sympathy was rather favourable to Germany, but the misfortunes of France soon evoked a kindlier feeling of sympathy for a nation that had so often acted in co-operation with England in European affairs. At the outset of the war, the

---

* Speech at Aylesbury, July 13, 1866.

British Government demanded guarantees from both the belligerent Powers that they would respect the neutrality of Belgium and Luxemburg, and pledged itself to join with either Power in the defence of these States if the territories were violated by the other. Another side-issue of the war was the repudiation by Russia of the clauses of the Treaty of Paris (1856), which limited her rights of sovereignty in the Black Sea. Great Britain protested against the claim of a State to abrogate a Treaty without the consent of the other signatories, but as war with Russia was out of the question, a conference in London agreed to the abandonment of the " Black Sea clauses," the Sultan being at the same time given the right to open the Dardanelles to the warships of friendly Powers should need arise. A special interest attaches to the settlement of the Alabama case, as the first example of the resort to arbitration between two great Powers. By the Treaty of Washington (May, 1871) it was agreed that the " Alabama claims " should be submitted to a commission of five members, nominated by the Queen, the President of the United States, the King of Italy, the President of the Swiss Republic, and the Emperor of Brazil. The commissioners met at Geneva, and after hearing evidence awarded the United States a sum of a little over three million, as against the original claim of £9,500,000. Valuable as was the precedent set by this appeal to arbitration, it was not carried through without costing the ministry some loss of popularity. Except for minor troubles connected with the extension of the Russian Empire in Central Asia, the last year of Gladstone's ministry passed tranquilly as far as foreign affairs were concerned. A feeling in the country that the policy of non-intervention had been carried too far, and that Great Britain had lost caste in the eyes of Europe, was one of the causes of the defeat of the ministry in the election at the beginning of 1874.

The first two years of Disraeli's ministry were years of comparative tranquillity in Europe. In the spring of 1875 German military opinion, alarmed at the rapidity with which France was recovering from the disaster of 1871, was inclined to press Bismarck to pick a quarrel with France, that she might be more completely crushed. Rumours of this intention were in circulation, and Queen Victoria joined the Czar in an appeal to the German Emperor to restrain his ministers. It is on the whole improbable that Bismarck ever seriously contemplated an attack on France, but the intervention of the sovereigns of Great Britain and Russia aroused his strong resentment.

French engineering won a notable triumph in the completion of the Suez Canal in 1869. When the project of a Canal through the Isthmus of Suez was first mooted, Palmerston strongly opposed it, partly on the ground that England, as the greatest sea-power, would inevitably be involved in the affairs of Egypt, since the Canal, if constructed, would become her main route to India. But the advantages to the world, and specially to Great Britain, of a shorter route to the east outweighed the risks that were involved. In November, 1875, Disraeli caused a sensation in Europe by purchasing, for five million pounds, the Khedive's shares in the Suez Canal Company, so giving to Great Britain the practical control of the Canal. Before this transaction was completed, the short-lived tranquillity of Europe was threatened by fresh troubles in the Ottoman Empire, from the consideration of which Great Britain could not hold aloof.

The Eastern Question (1875-80).

In the summer of 1875 a revolt broke out in the Turkish provinces of Bosnia and Herzegovina, not entirely unconnected with a visit paid by the Austrian Emperor to Dalmatia in the spring. Great Britain supported the Austrian minister, Count Andrassy, in his efforts to secure from the Porte reforms in its administration, but while negotiations dragged on the area of disturbance broadened. In May, 1876, the French and German consuls at Salonica were murdered by a Mussulman mob, and, soon after, Serbia and Montenegro declared war on Turkey. An attempt by Bismarck, acting in conjunction with Russia and Austria, to bring pressure on Turkey failed through the refusal of the British Government to co-operate, and the prospect of Russian intervention began to arouse the old anti-Russian feeling in England. Just at this stage, news reached England of atrocities in Bulgaria by Turkish irregular forces, and Gladstone, emerging from his retirement, stirred the nation by his pamphlet on ' The Bulgarian Horrors,' and appealed for the expulsion of the Turk, " bag and baggage " from the provinces he had so long misgoverned. The foreign secretary, Lord Derby, whose antipathy to Russia was less strong than that of his chief, addressed a stern remonstrance to the Turkish Government, warning it that British sympathy was being alienated by "the lamentable occurrences in Bulgaria." Meanwhile, the success of the Turkish army in Serbia threatened the complete subjection of the little kingdom, and Russia demanded an armistice.

A futile conference at Constantinople followed on an aggressive speech by Lord Beaconsfield at the Guildhall in November, and in April, 1877, Russia declared war on Turkey. The early successes of Russia were followed by a check at Plevna, and it was not till the beginning of 1878 that the Russian armies arrived at the gates of Constantinople. On January 23, the British fleet was ordered to the Dardanelles, and a supplementary estimate of six millions was voted by the House of Commons. Lord Carnarvon, the Colonial Secretary, resigned office owing to disapproval of these warlike measures. At the end of the month an armistice was signed by the two combatant Powers and in February the British fleet passed the Dardanelles and anchored ten miles from Constantinople. The Treaty of San Stefano was concluded in March, and the British Government joined with Austria in demanding that it should be submitted to a European Conference. A reply by Russia reserving to herself the right to accept or reject the decisions of the conference brought Great Britain and Russia to the verge of war. Lord Derby resigned the foreign secretaryship at this stage, and was succeeded by Lord Salisbury. In the country, the " jingo " feeling was strong, and a London mob broke the windows of Mr. Gladstone's house.

The feature of the Treaty of San Stefano to which the British Government specially objected was the creation of a " Big Bulgaria " reaching to the Aegean, and including practically the whole of Macedonia. At the end of May, Lord Salisbury negotiated a secret agreement with Russia, by which this big Bulgaria was divided, the southern part, with Macedonia, remaining under Turkish rule. In the following month, the British ministers made a secret treaty with Turkey, by which Great Britain engaged to defend the Asiatic provinces of the Ottoman Empire, and received Cyprus as a " place of arms." In return, the Sultan gave

the usual futile promise to introduce reforms into the
Armenian provinces of the Empire. These secret
arrangements cleared the ground for the Congress of
Berlin, at which Lord Beaconsfield and Lord Salisbury
represented Great Britain. Some difficult questions still remained for discussion, and at one stage
in the negotiations the British delegates threatened
to withdraw. But after a month of deliberation a
settlement was arrived at, which Russia, exhausted
by the war, was obliged to accept. In accordance
with a secret arrangement made with Russia before
the outbreak of the war, Austria occupied Bosnia and
Herzegovina, thereby extending the area of her influence in the Balkans. Southern Bulgaria was converted into the province of Eastern Roumelia, under
a Christian governor nominated by the Sultan, while
northern Bulgaria became autonomous ; and Roumania,
Serbia, and Montenegro were granted full independence.
Beaconsfield announced to the crowds at Whitehall
that he had brought back " Peace with honour."

In the light of all that has happened since, it is easy
to see that the Treaty of Berlin was a misfortune to
Europe. Instead of making a bold effort to settle,
once for all, the problem of the Balkans, the Powers,
hampered by mutual jealousy and distrust, fell back
upon a patchwork solution that condemned Macedonia
to thirty years more of Turkish misrule, left Bulgarian
aspirations unsatisfied, sowed the seeds of hostility
between Austria and Serbia, and committed Great
Britain to the task of bolstering up Turkish misrule in
Asia. Worst of all, it gave time for Germany to abandon
her attitude of indifference to Balkan questions. Like
the Congress of Vienna sixty-three years before, the
Congress of Berlin lacked the courage and disinterested-
ness that were needed to effect a lasting solution of the

problems with which it had to deal, and the history of
South Eastern Europe ever since has been the history
of the efforts of the Balkan States to set aside the
results of the Congress. Seven years after the Congress,
Eastern Roumelia declared its union with Bulgaria,
and it is a curious comment on the San Stefano proposals that the union was warmly supported by Great
Britain and strongly resented by Russia. Our guarantee
of the integrity of the Asiatic provinces of the Ottoman
Empire did not prevent the Sultan from perpetrating
the Armenian massacres, and the patronage of the
Turkish Government passed gradually into the hands
of Germany. In 1878, as in 1853, we had " put our
money on the wrong horse."

Roumania was rewarded for the help she had given
to the Russian cause by being compelled to cede Bess-
arabia to Russia, receiving in return the desolate
province of the Dobrudja inhabited chiefly by
Turks and Bulgarians. To the protests of the
Roumanian delegates Beaconsfield could only reply
that " in politics ingratitude is often the reward of
the greatest services." Two matters left unsettled
at Berlin occupied the attention of the British Government in the following years. Great Britain had from
the beginning of its history supported the Greek kingdom, and in 1863, when Prince George of Denmark
succeeded as King of the Hellenes, had shown her goodwill by ceding to Greece the Ionian Islands, which had been
left in her possession at the end of the Napoleonic
wars. At the Congress of Berlin, the claims of Greece
to a rectification of her frontier were recognized, largely
through the influence of Lord Salisbury, though her
demand for Crete was refused. Montenegro was also
granted an extension of territory, including two Albanian
districts of which she was unable to secure possession,

the resistance of the Albanians being secretly encouraged by the Turkish Government. Both these
questions remained unsettled when Gladstone succeeded
Beaconsfield as Prime Minister in 1880. His well-
known sympathy with Greece and Montenegro showed
itself in a determined effort to secure for both these
States the rights that had been given them at Berlin.
At a Conference held at Berlin in June, 1880, the Powers
unanimously agreed to "advise" the Porte to grant an
extension of Greek territory and to cede the Port of
Dulcigno to Montenegro in lieu of the Albanian districts.
The dilatoriness of the Turkish Government led to
preparations for a naval demonstration, and the seizure
of Smyrna by the allied fleets, and when it was
clear that the British Government meant business,
the Porte agreed to the cession of Dulcigno, and a few
months later, accepted a rectification of the frontier
that gave Greece Thessaly and part of Epirus. The
Montenegrins have ever since held Gladstone in grate-
ful remembrance.

From this time, Great Britain played a subordinate
part in the Near East, where the rivalry of Austria
and Russia was acute till Bulgarian "ingratitude"
led Russian statesmen to turn their attention towards
Central Asia, where Russian expansion led to constant
friction with Great Britain, and to the Far East, where
the extension of Russian influence in China and Corea
ultimately led to the war with Japan. After the
acquisition of Egypt, Great Britain had no longer the
same motive for acting as the protector of the Ottoman
Empire, and the Armenian atrocities of Abdul Hamid II.
alienated the sympathy of the majority of the British
people. Towards the end of the century, the German
Emperor made a successful effort to cultivate friendly
relations with the Sultan, whose undeveloped Asiatic

territories seemed to offer scope for German capital and enterprise.

THE EXPANSION OF EUROPE (1880-1900).

The Congress of Berlin may be said to close the chapter of European history that opened with the Congress of Vienna. Henceforth the relations of the Powers were affected less by internal European questions than by the world-wide struggle for colonies and markets. It was not on the Rhine and the Danube but in Tunis, Egypt, Nigeria, Manchuria, that the Chancelleries of Europe now found the centre of gravity of their diplomacy. The reasons for this change belong to the general history of Europe ; its results on British foreign policy were far-reaching. However detached we might be from the internal politics of Europe, the protection of our imperial interests and trade routes brought us into contact, and not seldom into collision, with the colonial aspirations of the other Powers. In particular, we were more than once involved in dangerous controversies with France and with Russia, the final settlement of which was only reached in the first decade of the present century. On the other hand, our relations with Germany, except for some inevitable friction now and then, continued fairly friendly till nearly the end of the century.

It was in Africa that European expansion found its chief sphere of activity. The "Monroe Doctrine" precluded the Powers of Europe from establishing spheres of influence in the New world, and the vast undeveloped resources of the "Dark Continent" attracted the attention of statesmen. In 1876, Leopold II. of Belgium founded the "International Association for the Exploration and Civilization of Africa," and thus laid the foundation of the Congo Free State.

At the Congress of Berlin, Lord Salisbury and Bismarck are said to have hinted to the French envoy that no objection would be raised by Great Britain or Germany to a French occupation of Tunis. Bismarck's object may have been to turn the attention of French statesmen from the idea of a war of revenge to colonial enterprize ; whether he foresaw that the French annexation of Tunis, which took effect in 1881, would arouse the hostility of Italy and so enable him to bring her into alliance with Germany and Austria, is more doubtful.

While France was occupied with Tunis, Great Britain became involved in a much more complicated struggle in Egypt. Ismail Pasha, Khedive of Egypt, had by his extravagance brought Egypt to the verge of bankruptcy, and as Egyptian bonds were held chiefly in England and France, the two Governments undertook the joint control of Egyptian finances in 1876. This " Dual Control " soon grew into a general supervision of Egyptian administration, and in 1879 Ismail was deposed by the Sultan, and Tewfik Pasha set up as Khedive in his place. The increase of foreign control led to a rise of a party in Egypt with the war cry of " Egypt for the Egyptians," and a leader was found in an Egyptian officer, Arabi Bey. Confusion increased in Egypt, and the fall of the French minister Gambetta, who was prepared to take the lead in intervention, left the chief responsibility for meeting the situation in the hands of the British Government. Gladstone was anxious to avoid isolated action, and it was only when all efforts to secure united action had failed that the British Government was obliged to act alone. An attempt by Arabi to fortify Alexandria led to the bombardment of the town by the British fleet (July, 1882), and in September the Egyptian army was defeated at Tel-el-Kebir, and Cairo surrendered to a force of British cavalry. France had refused to join in the campaign or allow Italy to do so, but in France, and throughout Europe, the action of Great Britain was strongly criticised. Gladstone tried to dissipate this hostility by assuring the Powers that the British occupation was only temporary, and that when order had been restored the British forces would be withdrawn. There is no doubt that the pledge was sincerely given, but the restoration of order proved a longer task than had been expected, and having accepted responsibility for the well-being of Egypt, circumstances obliged us to remain.

Of these circumstances the most important was the revolt of the Soudan, where a leader had arisen claiming to be a Moslem Messiah, " El Mahdi," as his followers called him. After an unsuccessful attempt by the Egyptian Government to suppress the rising, the British authorities determined on the evacuation of the Soudan, and General Gordon was sent, in 1884, to bring away the Egyptian garrisons. The story of the events that followed cannot be told here ; nor is it possible to discuss the extent of the responsibility of the Home government for the final disaster, when in January, 1885, just as a relief force was pushing its way up the Nile, Khartoum fell. The Soudan was abandoned to years of anarchy and oppression, and the British Government incurred the obligation of restoring it to Egypt before our army of occupation could be withdrawn from that country.

The Egyptian question was for some years the predominant issue in British foreign policy, but before the fall of the Gladstone ministry, a grave crisis elsewhere nearly led to war with Russia. The Russian Government, taking advantage of English entanglements in Egypt, had been pushing its boundaries in

Central Asia nearer to the frontiers of Afghanistan, and in March, 1885, a collision between Russian and Afghan troops took place at the frontier town of Penjdeh. Great indignation was felt in England at this affront, and the concessions by which the Cabinet preserved peace played no small part in securing the defeat of the Ministry a few weeks later. In the end, the action of Russia tended to strengthen the Indian frontier, by showing the Amir of Afghanistan that he had more to fear from Russia than from Great Britain. As the result of long-drawn-out negotiations, the frontier-line between Russia and Afghanistan was finally fixed in 1887.

During the last fifteen years of the century, the foreign policy of Great Britain was guided by Lord Salisbury, except for the brief periods during which Lord Rosebery was foreign secretary (1886, 1892-5)—and even these years were marked by no break in the continuity of our foreign policy, in regard to which Lord Rosebery was in fundamental agreement with the Conservative leader. One of the most important services that Lord Salisbury did was to lift foreign affairs out of the sphere of party contest. He had served a long apprenticeship in political life, and was always a little detached from party associations. He gradually came to exercise a degree of authority over foreign policy such as no minister of the Crown had done since the days of Palmerston. After the fall of Bismarck, in 1890, he became the recognized leader of European diplomacy, and to his sagacity and influence the maintenance of peace in Europe during the last decade of the century was largely due.

While England was occupied with Egypt, Germany had been staking out claims in Africa and elsewhere, and by 1884 the two countries were involved in a number of disputes, the settlement of which was rendered more difficult by hot-heads on both sides. The German Colonial Secretary inaugurated a press campaign against England, while the Gladstone government was accused by the advocates of a policy of imperial expansion, of neglecting to support legitimate British claims. In 1885, the German Protectorate of Zanzibar was recognized by the British Government, and a struggle between the British East Africa Company and the German East Africa Company was temporarily settled in 1886. A diplomatic controversy also arose in regard to South Africa, where the German South-West African Colony was established in 1883 by the hoisting of the German flag at Angra Pequena, Walfisch Bay alone falling to the share of Great Britain. Strong dissatisfaction was felt at the Cape at what was regarded as the sacrifice of British interests in this region. An attempt by Germany to secure a foothold at St. Lucia Bay, on the other flank of British South Africa, was frustrated owing to the pressure brought to bear on the Home Government by Colonial opinion. In the same year (1885) the British Government resisted successfully the attempt of the German authorities to annex Pondoland, and by the annexation of Bechuanaland, and of Burmah, forestalled possible dangers from Germany and France. An agreement was also made with Germany fixing the frontier line of the new German colony of the Cameroons. Meanwhile, the acquisition by Germany of Samoa, New Guinea and other territories in the Australasian area alarmed the Australian colonies, and greatly stimulated the movement for federation which bore fruit in 1900 in the formation of the Commonwealth of Australia.

An impartial examination of the facts will not bear out the accusation that Great Britain deliberately set

itself to frustrate Germany's legitimate colonial aspirations. It would be too much to say that English
public opinion wholly endorsed the welcome that
Gladstone offered to Germany as "a friend and ally in
the spread of civilization," but where our Imperial
interests were not menaced, we did not place any obstacles in the way of German expansion. It must be
remembered that the trade of our Crown colonies was
open to all nations, while the German protective system
aimed at securing a monopoly of trade in her colonies
for her own citizens. It cannot be denied that the
position of Germany was a difficult one. Coming late
into the field, she found the most desirable parts of
the world already appropriated, and her desire for
" a place in the sun " could only be realized by pushing
with side and with shoulder in a way that other nations
resented.

After 1886, the expansion of Europe slowed down,
and the relations between Great Britain and Germany
improved for a time. In 1887, Lord Salisbury refused
to assent to vague claims of Portugal to Mashonaland,
and in the following year our relations with France
were affected by controversy about Madagascar.

The year 1890 was in many ways an important one
in regard to foreign affairs. The fall of Bismarck
removed from the leadership of German affairs a
statesman whose attitude towards Great Britain had
not been marked by great friendliness, and it was
hoped that the young Emperor would adopt a more
friendly policy. An important Treaty was concluded
between the two countries defining the frontiers of
German East Africa and South-West Africa, and
transferring Heligoland to Germany. The dissatisfaction expressed in both countries is perhaps the best
evidence of the substantial justice of the solution

arrived at, and the cession of Heligoland was a convincing evidence of the desire of the British Government to meet legitimate German desires. In the same year, agreements were concluded with France about Madagascar, Nigeria, and Zanzibar, and with Portugal, after an ultimatum had been sent to the Portuguese Government, about Rhodesia and Nyassaland.

The Liberal government that assumed office in 1892 was only involved in one serious colonial controversy. The expansion of French dominion in Indo-China brought France into collision with Siam, and for some time relations between the British Government and France were severely strained. In the end, Siam was retained as a " buffer-state," and the frontier lines were finally deliminated in 1896.

A more important step was the recognition by Great Britain of the new status of Japan, with which Power a treaty was made in 1894. Soon after, the outbreak of war between China and Japan brought into fresh prominence the problem of the Far East. When Russia, France, and Germany combined to deprive Japan of the fruits of her victory, and occupied important spheres of influence on the Chinese coast, Great Britain secured a lease of Wei-Hai-Wei " so long as Russia was in occupation of Port Arthur." The return of Lord Salisbury to the Premiership (with which he also held the Secretaryship for foreign affairs) in 1895 coincided with a new period of stress and strain in British foreign relations. A dispute with Venezuela with regard to the boundaries of British Guiana, which Lord Salisbury refused to submit to arbitration, led to an intemperate dispatch from President Cleveland, which might have brought about war between the United States and Great Britain if the commonsense of both countries had not come to the rescue. Lord

Salisbury offered to lay the British case before a boundary commission "without prejudice to British rights." A Commission was appointed in 1897, and gave an award two years later that constituted an almost complete vindication of British claims.

While the Venezuela controversy was at an acute stage, the "Jameson Raid" gave our Foreign Office grave anxiety. The story of South Africa is too long to tell here, and it belongs to the history of colonial rather than foreign policy, but the raid had one important consequence. The acquisition by Germany of territories in South Africa had led British statesmen to suspect that she intended to intrigue with the Boer Republics, and these suspicions seemed to be confirmed by a telegram sent by the Kaiser to President Kruger, congratulating him on repelling the attack "without appealing to the help of friendly Powers." Wholly indefensible as the raid had been, the intervention of Germany was strongly resented in this country, and it is not too much to say that we may date from this event the permanent alienation between the two nations that led in the end to the arrangement of the European Powers in two hostile groups between which an armed peace was preserved only by mutual fear.

One result of this alienation was the impotence of Europe when the Armenian massacres of 1895-6, showed the folly of expecting that the Turkish leopard could change his spots. Great Britain had a special responsibility for Asiatic Turkey under the Cyprus Convention, but Lord Rosebery and Lord Salisbury both believed that any attempt at independent action would bring on a European war, and the unfortunate Armenians were left to their fate. In the following year, Lord Salisbury was able to do more effective service in the Cretan question, in regard to which

Great Britain succeeded in persuading the Powers to act together. In consequence, Greece was saved from the worst consequences of her rash attack on Turkey, and Crete secured autonomy under the joint protection of the Powers.

The history of British foreign policy now brings us back to Egypt. In 1890 the British Government offered to evacuate Egypt on condition that Great Britain was given the right to intervene in case of serious danger to the peace and security of that country The refusal of France and Russia to assent to this condition led to the abandonment of the proposal. During the years that followed, General Kitchener was gradually training the Egyptian army in preparation for the reconquest of the Soudan, and in 1896 the Egyptian forces advanced to Dongola. Next year a further advance was made, and in September, 1898 the Anglo-Egyptian victory of Omdurman finally broke the power of the Khalifa, and restored the Soudan to Egypt.

France had resented the British occupation of Egypt, and the withdrawal of Egyptian forces from the Soudan awakened in French statesmen a desire to gain a foothold on the Upper Nile. If Egypt had surrendered her sovereignty over the Soudan, there seemed no legal reason why other Powers should not stake out claims there, as Great Britain had done in Uganda (1894). In 1895 Sir Edward Grey warned the French Government that England would regard a French expedition to the Upper Nile as " an unfriendly act," and the danger of such an expedition was one of the chief motives for the advance of 1896-8. Meanwhile, Major Marchand had started from the French Congo, and after nearly two years of struggling through swamps, forests and rapids, arrived at Fashoda in July, 1898, and there hoisted the French flag. Hearing of this, Kitchener sailed up the Nile, and the two men met in the heart of Africa. Marchand refused to retire, and the question was referred to the two Home governments. Feeling ran high on both sides of the Channel, and only the recall of Marchand by the French Government averted the outbreak of war. In 1899 an Anglo-French agreement defined the southern frontiers of Anglo Egyptian territory, and Egypt was thus saved from the danger of losing control over the headwaters of the river on which her life depended.

The closing years of the century were marked by a notable effort to foster international peace, when, at the invitation of the Czar, a conference met at the Hague to consider the question of reduction of armaments (May, 1899). No practical scheme of disarmament could be devised, Germany in particular refusing to limit her right to provide for her own protection, but, largely through the influence of the British delegate, Lord Pauncefote, a Tribunal was set up to which international questions would be submitted, and rules of procedure, &c., were drafted.

Scarcely had the Hague Conference completed its work before the British Empire found itself at war with the two Dutch Republics in South Africa. The war, which broke out in October, 1899, proved a sterner task than had been anticipated. The sympathies of most European Powers were with the Boers, Italy alone remaining friendly to Great Britain—and, indeed, it is probable that but for our unchallenged naval supremacy Germany would have led the other Powers in a policy of intervention. The realization of her impotence was one of the chief causes of the German Naval Act of 1900, by which the German Empire definitely entered the arena as a great naval Power, and thus opened a new and sinister chapter in the history of Anglo-German relations, since it was impossible for Great Britain, whose very existence as a world-power depended on her fleet, to allow her naval supremacy to be endangered.

The death of Queen Victoria, on January 22, 1901, may be said to mark, for England, the close of the century, with the last sixty years of which she had been closely associated. During the later part of her life, her influence over foreign policy had been very slight, but her intimate association with the other crowned heads of Europe was not without its value as an asset for international peace. Her death removed the last influence that made for the maintenance of friendly relations with Germany, and Lord Salisbury's retirement six months later, as soon as the Treaty of Vereeniging had brought the South African war to an end, transferred the control of British foreign policy into the hands of Lord Lansdowne (1902-6), and then of Sir Edward Grey.

The close of the century left Great Britain in the position of " splendid isolation " that had for long been the guiding principle of our foreign policy. While seeking to cultivate friendly relations with all the European Powers, we had refused to entangle ourselves with alliances, and maintained a middle position between the Triple Alliance and the new Entente that had grown up between France and Russia. Our relations with Russia were correct rather than cordial, with France they were gradually growing more friendly. With Italy alone we remained, throughout the whole period, on completely friendly terms. With the opening of the present century the competition in armaments between the great Powers grew more acute, and the prospects of international peace became steadily less hopeful. J. H. B. MASTERMAN.

BIBLIOGRAPHY.

As there is, as yet, no adequate history of British foreign relations during the last century, the subject must be studied in the general histories of the period, and in the biographies and memoirs of statesmen. Useful general histories are :—

' The Cambridge Modern History,' vols. x., xi., xii.

' The Political History of England ' (Longmans), vols. xi.' and xii.

' The Development of the European Nations, 1870-1900 , Holland Rose.

Among short biographies, the following may be recommended :—

' Pitt,' Lord Rosebery.

' George Canning,' Marriott.

' Palmerston,' ' Beaconsfield,' and ' Lord Salisbury ' in the " Queen's Prime Ministers Series."

The following larger biographies and memoirs are of special importance :—

' Life of Gladstone,' by Lord Morley.

' Life of Palmerston,' Daling and Ashley.

' Memoirs of an ex-Minister,' Lord Malmesbury.

' The Third Salisbury Administration,' Whates.

' The Eastern Question,' Duke of Argyle.

For International Affairs generally, Sir Edward Hertslet's ' Map of Europe by Treaty ' is indispensable; and for the earlier and later parts of the period respectively, ' The Memoirs of Prince Metternich ' and Seignobos, ' Political History of Contemporary Europe ' are valuable.

BRITISH FOREIGN POLICY IN THE TWENTIETH CENTURY.

THE South African war marks not only the end of a century but the abandonment of the policy which Great Britain had pursued throughout its course. During the three generations which had elapsed since the downfall of Napoleon she had endeavoured to hold aloof from continental entanglements, finding ample scope for her energies in domestic reform and in the consolidation of her ever-widening Empire. Not that she turned a blind eye to the twin forces of democracy and nationality which were fashioning a new Europe ; for the names of Canning, Palmerston, and Gladstone hold a high place in the story of the emancipation of other lands. Nor could she boast of unbroken peace ; for her dread of Russia led her to Sebastopol, and she shewed her teeth to the United States in 1861 and to France in 1898. But while sharp differences of opinion divided the country in regard to particular steps, as they divided Cobden from Palmerston and Gladstone from Beaconsfield, the nation was at one in desiring to keep its hands unbound, to remain master of its fate, to pursue the even tenor of its way behind the rampart of the sea, to trust to its fleet for the security which Continental Powers sought in alliances and conscript armies. Though mistakes were sometimes committed, this policy of conditional isolation and watchful independence was well adapted to secure the honour and maintain the interests of the country, until the dawning light of the twentieth century revealed unsuspected dangers and suggested the reconsideration of fundamental principles. The story of this reconsideration and of the dramatic changes in the orientation of Imperial policy to which it led forms the subject of this chapter.

I. The Alliance with Japan.

The international position of Great Britain on the eve of the Boer War was not altogether satisfactory. France smarted with the wound of Fashoda, the United States remembered Venezuela, and our embittered rivalry with Russia had recently been extended to the northern coasts of China. And now the prolonged struggle in South Africa intensified existing enmities and created new ones. The world troubled itself but little about the rights and wrongs, the provocations and counter-provocations, of the dragging controversy which preceded the appeal to arms. It was enough that the greatest of Empires was engaged in conflict with two backward and sparsely populated Republics, endowed with unlimited stores of mineral wealth. The Emperor Francis Joseph remarked at a diplomatic reception at the Hofburg, " In this contest I am on the side of England " ; but, speaking broadly, the war was thoroughly unpopular outside the British Empire and lowered our moral prestige throughout the world. In this soil of critical or hostile sentiment, whether old or new, interested or disinterested, it was natural enough that plans of collective action, or at any rate of collective pressure, should arise. The conversations that took place between France, Germany and Russia while our armies were engaged overseas have never been officially disclosed. It seems clear, however, that the initiative was taken by Muravieff, the Russian Foreign Minister, on a visit to Paris after the outbreak of war, and that the scheme collapsed when the Kaiser proposed the condition that the three Powers should mutually guarantee the integrity of their territories.*

* See Lémonon, L'Europe et la politique Britannique, 196-200 ; André Mévil, De la paix de Francfort à la Conférence d'Algésiras, chapter 1 ; and Reventlow, Deutschland's Auswärtige Politik.

Though nothing came of them, the subterranean rumblings left behind them a certain alarm, and created a sub-conscious feeling that it was dangerous for us to move through a crowd of scowling or averted faces without a single powerful friend. In no quarter was there any longer a desire to widen still further the boundaries of our far-flung Empire. The era of acquisition had melted into the era of conservation. Henceforth peace was the greatest of British interests.

The first step on the path that led away from isolation was the Anglo-Japanese treaty, signed in January, 1902. Its conclusion was hardly less of a surprise to the British Empire than to the rest of the world. King Edward himself, according to Sir Sidney Lee, was at first startled by the new departure. Yet the ground had been slowly and to a large extent unwittingly prepared. The emergence of Japan from mediæval twilight into a powerful modern State had naturally inspired her with a desire to abolish the treaty rights which deprived her of all power over foreign residents and prevented her from raising her tariff. For some years the Powers refused her request ; but in 1894 Lord Rosebery's Ministry surrendered the ex-territorial rights of British subjects and thereby recognized her as a civilized State. For the first time the fortunes of Europeans were submitted to the jurisdiction of an Oriental Power. The testimonial was highly prized for its own sake and for the example which it set. By 1899 the last shackles were removed, and Japan took her place, in law not less than in fact, beside the other great Powers of the world.

To the positive homage thus rendered by Great Britain a negative service was quickly added. The war with China arising out of conflicting claims in Korea resulted in a sweeping victory for the island empire ; but the ink on the treaty of peace was scarcely dry before Russia, France and Germany peremptorily ordered the conqueror to surrender the Liao-Tung peninsula on the ground that the possession of Port Arthur threatened the independence of Pekin. Japan had no alternative but to submit ; but she naturally harboured no friendly feelings for the Powers who had snatched from her the choicest fruits of victory. Her anger with the ringleader was increased to boiling-point when Russia two years later appropriated the coveted ice-free port. That Great Britain stood aloof from the robber band had been a source of sincere satisfaction ; and the indignation which the seizure of Port Arthur aroused throughout the British Empire forged a new bond between London and Tokio. The tightening grip of the Russian bear on Northern China caused the keenest apprehension to both Powers—to Great Britain on account of her trade, to Japan on account of Korea. After the suppression of the Boxer revolt Russia invited China to resume the government of Manchuria, now occupied by Russian troops, under Russian protection. The spectre of a war for the hegemony of the Far East began to loom on the horizon, and Japan determined to look round for friends.

The posthumous publication of the Memoirs of Viscount Hayashi, Ambassador to the Court of St. James's, has lifted the veil from the origins of the Anglo-Japanese alliance. The Elder Statesmen of Japan differed as to how to meet the danger which they all recognized. Prince Ito desired a frank discussion with Russia herself, and proceeded on an unofficial but fruitless visit to St. Petersburg with this object.*

---

* The conversations are summarised by Prince Trubetzkoi Russland als Grossmacht, 58-60.

The larger party was convinced that a satisfactory agreement with Russia was impossible, and preferred an alliance with her rival. In the spring of 1901 Baron von Eckardstein, German Chargé d'Affaires in London, paid Hayashi several visits and suggested a triple alliance between Japan, Great Britain and Germany, adding that the leading British ministers and " two of the most distinguished dignitaries of the German Empire " favoured it. The Ambassador jumped at the idea, and obtained permission to sound the British Government. Lord Lansdowne approved the suggestion of an agreement between Great Britain and Japan, adding that it need not be confined to those two countries. A little later, however, he remarked, " We think it will be best to negotiate with you first, and then we can invite Germany to join in the negotiations and come into the alliance." Germany, however, was not invited, and Reventlow declares that Eckardstein's proposal was unauthorized, as Germany had no desire to join an anti-Russian league or to bind herself to England. Long discussions took place between Lord Lansdowne and Hayashi, Japan declining the British proposal to extend the terms of the treaty to India. The preamble and the governing articles are as follows :-

" The Governments of Great Britain and Japan, actuated solely by a desire to maintain the *status quo* and general peace in the extreme East, being moreover especially interested in maintaining the territorial integrity of the Empire of China and the Empire of Korea, and in securing equal opportunities in those countries for the commerce and industry of all nations, hereby agree as follows :—

" Art. I. The High Contracting Parties, having mutually recognized the independence of China and of Korea, declare themselves to be entirely uninfluenced by any aggressive tendencies in either country. Having in view, however, their special interests, of which those of Great Britain relate principally to China, while Japan, in addition to the interests which she possesses in China, is interested in a peculiar degree politically, as well as commercially and industrially, in Korea, the High Contracting Parties recognise that it will be admissible for either of them to take such measures as may be indispensable in order to safeguard those interests if threatened either by the aggressive action of any other Power, or by disturbances arising in China or Korea, and necessitating the intervention of either of the High Contracting Parties for the protection of the lives and property of its subjects.

"Art. II. If either Great Britain or Japan, in the defence of their respective interests as above described, should become involved in war with another Power, the other High Contracting Party will maintain a strict neutrality, and use its efforts to prevent other Powers from joining in hostilities against its ally.

"Art. III. If, in the above event, any other Power or Powers should join in hostilities against that ally, the other High Contracting Party will come to its assistance, and will conduct the war in common, and make peace in mutual agreement with it."

The treaty was received with satisfaction in both countries. The admission of Japan to alliance on equal terms with a great European Power gave her a position which had never been attained by any Oriental State. In the second place it virtually assured her that in the event of war with Russia her ally would keep the ring and she would only have to meet a single foe. The advantage to Great Britain was less direct; but the addition of the growing armaments of Japan to our potential strength in the Far East was a solid gain. The new allies might well feel that their joint resources would be a match for any hostile combination, and would be able to defend the commercial and political interests which Russian aggression appeared likely to threaten.

The treaty was concluded for five years; but in 1904 the expected conflict began, and in 1905, while the war was still in progress, a new treaty of wider scope was substituted, and two new principles of the utmost importance were introduced. In the first place each was to come to the assistance of the other if attacked by a single Power. In the second, the scope of the agreement was extended to embrace India. The inequality of advantage was thus redressed. The aim of the alliance was now officially defined as " the consolidation and maintenance of general peace in the regions of Eastern Asia and of India."

The agreement of 1905 was concluded for ten years; but before the term was reached a further important change was effected at the desire of Great Britain. The fourth Article of the pact as revised in 1911 runs as follows: " Should either High Contracting Party conclude a treaty of general arbitration with a third Power, it is agreed that nothing in this Agreement shall entail upon such Contracting Party an obligation to go to war with the Power with whom such treaty of arbitration is in force."* This clause removed the danger, implicit in the treaty of 1905, of our being involved in a war between Japan and the United States. The value of the compact to Great Britain was to be revealed in spectacular fashion in 1914, when her ally conquered Kiao-Chau and aided the British fleet to sweep the German flag from the Pacific.

* The three treaties are printed by Sir R. Douglas, Europe and the Far East, 418-20, 459-62.

II. The Entente with France.

Not long after the conclusion of an alliance with
Japan a task of far greater urgency and imporance
was taken in hand. Though peace had been maintained between Great Britain and France since 1815
and the two countries had fought side by side against
Russia, lasting relations of confidence had never been
established. Under Louis Philippe the entente of
Guizot and Aberdeen was shattered by the Spanish
marriages. Under Louis Napoleon the comradeship
of the Crimea was succeeded by the scare to which
the Volunteers owed their existence. In 1870 the
British people, while sympathizing with the sufferings
of the nation, condemned the provocative policy of its
ruler. Under the Third Republic the era of colonial
expansion, inaugurated by Jules Ferry, opened up a
new and boundless vista of controversy. The seizure
of Tunis, the fortification of Bizerta, the convict settle-
ments in New Caledonia, the occupation of the New
Hebrides, the rivalry in Nigeria, the coercion of Siam,
the exclusion of British trade from Madagascar, the
Newfoundland fisheries, above all the occupation of
Egypt—these thorny problems were continually prick-
ing the fingers of the diplomatists in Downing Street
and the Quai d'Orsai, and causing anxiety to the
friends of peace on both sides of the Channel. The
Marchand mission to the Upper Nile, despatched in
open defiance of Sir Edward Grey's solemn warning
in 1895, led to the sharpest tension. When Kitchener
marched south after Omdurman and ordered the French
force to quit Fashoda, peace hung upon a thread
The French fleet in the Mediterranean slipped past Gibraltar
at night, the Mayors of the Channel ports were ordered
to requisition churches and public buildings for hospitals,
and four millions were hurriedly spent on increasing

the store of munitions at Cherbourg. But when British opinion expressed itself in uncompromising terms, and Russia announced that she would not lend her aid in a war for the Upper Nile, the French ministry unconditionally surrendered. A few weeks later Sir Edmund Monson, the British ambassador, in a speech to the British Chamber of Commerce in Paris, complained of the policy of pinpricks and hinted plainly that it must stop. The embitterment of French feeling was intensified by the measureless anger aroused beyond the Channel by the handling of the Dreyfus case. While the wounds of humiliation were still raw, the Boer war provided an unrivalled opportunity for the expression of the hatred that had been accumulating for years in the heart of France. When Kruger fled from his country, he was received with ovations at Marseilles and Paris by the enemies of his enemy.

The danger to the peace of the world involved in the continual bickering of the two Powers had naturally led calmer spirits on both sides of the Channel to consider the possibility of removing its main causes. Lord Lyons, perhaps the weightiest of British Ambassadors, watched the beginning of the colonial friction with growing apprehension. Lord Lytton, though a social success, was powerless to arrest the process of embitterment. In 1894 Lord Dufferin, convinced that things were drifting from bad to worse, suggested to Hanotaux, the Foreign Minister, that the Foreign Offices should endeavour to settle their difficulties, with Egypt as the centre of the discussion. The two men, with their assistants, made an attempt; but the scheme was disapproved by both Governments and has never been revealed. Lord Salisbury, who returned to the Foreign Office in 1895, entertained no sanguine hopes of improvement, and his view was

shared and expressed by Dufferin's successor, Sir
Edmund Monson.

It was at the moment when the clouds were blackest,
in the critical weeks of the Fashoda crisis, that Delcassé
commenced that long tenure of the Foreign Office
which was to change the face of European politics.
The withdrawal from the Upper Nile was no more
agreeable to him than to other patriotic Frenchmen ;
but shortly after his appointment he remarked to a
friend that he hoped to remain in office long enough
to restore harmonious relations with Great Britain.
The same view had been expressed by a French ambassador two days after the surrender in the words,
" Once the difference about the Sudan is settled, nothing
stands in the way of a complete *entente* with England.''
The enemy was Germany, and he had no desire to
fight any one else.

Though Delcassé's attitude towards Great Britain
was very different from that of Hanotaux, he could
accomplish little while public opinion in both countries
was angry and suspicious. It was in this field that
work of enduring importance was accomplished by
Sir Thomas Barclay, a journalist and barrister, who
won for himself a distinct place in the political and
literary life of the capital, and whose ' Reminiscences '
have thrown welcome light on the making of the
entente. It occurred to him that it would be of service
to the good cause if the British Chambers of Commerce
were invited to meet in the French capital in 1900,
the year of his Presidency of the Chamber in Paris.
The British Foreign Office and the British Embassy
gave no assistance ; but the French Government was
sympathetic, and the meeting was a great success.
Though Kruger's visit took place shortly after, the
seed had been sown, and the gross caricatures of Queen

Victoria in the illustrated papers disappeared. But
no real advance was probable while Lord Salisbury's
influence was supreme, and Delcassé remarked to Sir
Thomas that it was hopeless to try to conciliate
England.

Lord Salisbury resigned on the conclusion of the
Boer War, and died not long afterwards. Lord Lans-
dówne, who had been Foreign Minister since 1900,
now gained a free hand and shewed himself desirous
of cordial relations. Moreover, King Edward's well-
known friendship for France introduced a new and
hopeful element into the sentiment of the two countries.
The extent of his influence in the formation of the
entente has been actively canvassed. In continental
countries, where the British Constitution is imperfectly
understood, there has been a natural tendency to ex-
aggerate the role of a man of magnetic personality,
keenly interested in foreign affairs and constantly
engaged in continental travel. "It was the King of
England," writes Tardieu, "who initiated and prepared the *rapprochement*."* To remove this mis-
apprehension his friend Lord Esher wrote an article
in the *Deutsche Revue* after his death, which may be
taken as authoritative† "The popular idea outside
the British Isles that King Edward moulded the foreign
policy of his country is pure illusion. He always
recognized that to initiate the policy of Great Britain
was the business of Ministers, and his function was to
criticize or approve it and finally to support it with
all his powers. This he performed with such clearness
of vision and supreme tact as to command not only
the gratitude of his own people but the admiration
of competent judges all over the world. It is ridiculous

* France and the Alliances.
† Republished in The Influence of Edward 7 and other Essays.

to suppose that the King initiated or planned the *entente* between Great Britain and France. But he cordially accepted and enthusiastically supported the policy. "

In May, 1903, the King paid his first official visit to Paris and was received with respect though without enthusiasm. In July President Loubet returned the compliment by a visit to London. In October the first-fruits of the harvest were gathered when a Treaty of Arbitration, the work of Sir Thomas Barclay and Baron d'Estournelles de Constant, was signed by which the two countries agreed to submit all disputes of a judicial character to the Hague Tribunal,—a pact which has been pertinently described as an interim manifesto of goodwill. The atmosphere had now cleared to such an extent that a discussion of controversial issues could be profitably undertaken. The two Foreign Ministers, aided by Paul Cambon, the ambassador in London, were busily engaged throughout the winter, and it was proved once again that with goodwill on both sides the thorniest problems can be solved. Success was rendered less difficult by the very magnitude of the field of controversy. However impossible it might seem to agree on particular issues in isolation, compromises might prove feasible as items in a balanced settlement. The diplomatic artists worked in large perspective, conscious that the removal of inflammable material throughout broad expanses of the world would far outweigh the renunciation of an ancient claim or the surrender of some glittering prospect.

" The immediate origin of the Entente," records Lord Cromer, " is to be found mainly in the local agitation existing at the time in Egypt. Egyptian finance was then in a flourishing condition ; but owing to the international fetters imposed in circumstances which had wholly ceased to exist, the country was unable to derive any real profit from the surplus funds. The position had, in fact, become intolerable. It was determined to make an effort to improve it. A high Egyptian official was sent to Paris to feel the pulse of the French Government. Simultaneously responsible Frenchmen had come to the conclusion that it was practically impossible for the British Government to redeem the pledge to evacuate Egypt. The British advances were therefore met in a friendly spirit."

The influence of France had been preponderant in Egypt since Napoleon, and the construction of the Suez Canal by de Lesseps added to her pride and her interests in the country. The Dual Control established by the British and French creditors of the Khedive Ismail seemed to promise a prolonged period of co-operation ; but when France declined to aid in the suppression of Arabi's revolt she lost her chance, and the British occupation began. Though labelled temporary it soon became clear that there was no prospect of evacuation, and the reconquest of the Sudan was an unmistakeable announcement of its permanence. In deciding not to fight for Fashoda France confessed to her defeat in the long struggle, and her obvious policy was to look elsewhere for compensation. Moreover, the British occupation offered first-rate security for the punctual payment of interest on the millions that she had invested. Accordingly, in the treaty of 1904 she promised not to obstruct the action of Great Britain by demanding a time limit for the occupation or in any other way, Great Britain for her part declaring that she had no intention of altering the political status of the country. Germany, Austria and Italy subsequently adhered to this arrangement, by which Great Britain regularized her position and secured a free hand in finance.

The recognition of British rule in Egypt was purchased by the recognition of French claims in Morocco. The position of that country, wedged in between her other colonial possessions, naturally prompted the desire to round off her vast African empire ; and the growing internal anarchy opened up prospects that in the land of the Moors might perchance be realized the ambitions that had been thwarted in the valley of the Nile. The long Algerian frontier needed orderly neighbours, and the rich iron deposits of the Atlas would prove a welcome resource in the race of armaments. British strategic and commercial interests were safeguarded by an agreement to forbid the erection of fortifications on the coast opposite Gibraltar, and to prevent differentiation in duties, taxes, railway and other charges for thirty years. Great Britain recognized that " it appertains to France, more particularly as a Power whose dominions are conterminous for a great distance with those of Morocco, to preserve order in that country, and to provide the assistance for the purpose of all administrative, economic, financial, and military reforms which it may require." As in the case of Egypt, the treaty disclaims all intention of altering the political status of the country.

The core of the Anglo-French agreement was the recognition of respective interests in Egypt and Morocco ; but the treaty also swept away the main causes of friction all over the world. The hoary dispute as to fishing rights off Newfoundland, a survival from the old French ascendancy in North America, was settled by buying out French interests. In the New Hebrides, which Australia claimed as within her sphere of influence while France urged their contiguity to New Caledonia, a condominium, the details of which were to be worked out later, replaced the anarchy in which

British and French settlers had lived. In Siam, across which the British from Burma and the French from Indo-China had glared at each other, spheres of in-fluence were arranged. Great Britain at last reconciled herself to the tariff in Madagascar, which had virtually killed her trade, and made some boundary concessions on the Gambia, in Guinea, and in the district of Lake Chad.

The Agreement has been aptly compared to a treaty of peace after a drawn war. Though Lord Rosebery expressed his hope that the country which holds Gibraltar might never have cause to regret having handed Morocco over to a great military Power, and Deschanel contended that better terms could have been won, the voice of criticism was drowned in the chorus of approval from both sides of the Channel. What each surrendered, declared Mr. Balfour, was scarcely a sacrifice; what each had gained was of enormous importance. Not only had the recurring danger of war been removed, but the position of the two Powers in face of rivals and possible enemies was immensely strengthened. For the one it marked a further departure from hazardous isolation; to the other it brought an accession of security only second in importance to the Russian alliance.

The good will that had produced the treaty quickly developed under the stress of events into a diplomatic *entente*. In the autumn of the same year the Russian fleet on its passage through the North Sea fired on some Hull fishermen and caused several casualties. In any case the situation created by the Russo-Japanese war was not without its difficulties, for France was allied with one of the combatants and Great Britain with the other. The outrage caused an explosion of wrath in England; but it was so obviously a mistake

that the British Government readily accepted French
mediation and submitted the matter to a Commission
of inquiry at Paris. The error of the Russian Admiral
was established, compensation was paid and the danger
passed away. The importance of removing the causes
of friction now began to be recognized, and it was obvious
that our friendship with France would only rest on
secure foundations when the atmosphere of suspicion
and hostility which had separated England and Russia
since the Crimean War had been dispelled. But before
this step could be taken, the intimacy of the Anglo-
French *entente* was revealed to the world in the first
of the diplomatic crises which shook Europe to its
foundations during the decade which preceded the
outbreak of the Great War.

Delcassé had bought British, Italian, and Spanish
recognition of French interests in Morocco ; but there
were other signatories of the Treaty of Madrid of 1880,
which governed its status, among them Germany,
whose trade was growing to considerable dimensions.
By a disastrous error of judgment he omitted to offer
a corresponding sop to the German Cerberus, and even
failed officially to inform the German Government of
the Moroccan agreement.* Its reception in official
Germany, however, was not unfriendly. " We have
no cause to apprehend that it is levelled against any
inidvidual Power," declared the Chancellor in the
Reichstag, " or that our substantial economic interests
in Morocco will be disregarded or injured." " We
shall have to take care that France fulfils her pledge
of the open door," echoed Prof. Schiemann in his

* André Mevil, who hotly defends Delcassé against all comers in
chapters 4 and 5 of his book, 'De la Paix de Francfort à la
Conférence d'Algésiras,' denies that he was guilty of neglect or
discourtesy to Germany ; but the consensus of opinion is against him
on this point.

weekly survey in the *Kreuz Zeitung* ; " we have nothing
to complain of if French policy does not deviate from
pacific penetration." Though she was not bound by
an agreement in regard to which she had not been
consulted, she had no quarrel with its professed principles. In the autumn a document was signed by
which Spain declared her adherence to the Anglo-
French treaty on Egypt and Morocco.

It appeared as if the new *entente* had a prosperous
voyage before it ; but the sky was quickly overcast.
Early in 1905 the French Minister set out for Fez with
a far-reaching programme of reforms to be carried
out by the aid of French loans. In the nerveless hands
of Sultan Abdul Aziz the kingdom had fallen into chaos,
and from the European point of view stood in urgent
need of guidance and re-organization. Before the
mission started the German Secretary of Legation at
Tangier informed the French Minister that his Government had not been consulted. Delcassé ignored the
hint, and in March the Kaiser landed from his yacht
at Tangier—" in pursuance of my advice," writes
Prince Bülow. In peremptory language he announced
that the Sultan was absolutely independent, that it
would not be wise to hurry reform, and that German
interests would be safeguarded. The speech, which
was naturally regarded as an exhortation to resist
French demands, was followed by an invitation from
the Sultan to the signatories of the Madrid Treaty to
a new Conference.

What had occurred to cause the sharp change in the
attitude of Germany ? The answer commonly given
in France and England is that the Kaiser had taken
advantage of the defeat of Russia to bully Russia's
ally and to strike a blow at the *entente*. But was that
the only reason ? German approval had been given

on the basis of the treaty declaration and Delcassé's personal assurances that no alteration of the political status of Morocco was intended. But in addition to the published agreements with Great Britain and Spain there were also secret treaties which were to come into operation " if the status quo can no longer be maintained." In that event it was agreed that Morocco should be partitioned between France and Spain, the latter to obtain the Mediterranean coast and the Atlantic districts facing Gibraltar, in order that the British fortress might not be confronted by the territory of a great military and naval Power. The secret clauses of the two treaties were only revealed to the world in November, 1911, in the columns of the *Matin* and the *Temps*. But as they were known to several people in London, Paris, and Madrid, and communicated to St. Petersburg, their existence, if not their details, was quickly discovered by Berlin. Indeed it was soon an open secret, for when the Franco-Spanish treaty was published in October, a Reuter telegram announced that it contained " a number of secret clauses." In ' Morocco in Diplomacy ' Mr. Morel has traced a large part of the misfortunes which have overwhelmed Europe to these clauses, which he believes to have embodied the real ambitions of their author. Prof. Gilbert Murray, on the other hand, in his defence of the policy of Sir Edward Grey, (though Sir Edward had, of course, no share in the work of 1904), maintains that there was nothing dishonourable in the secret, and that it was reasonable for the contracting parties to make alternative arrangements in the not improbable event of Morocco collapsing from internal weakness. Our moral judgment of the whole transaction will depend on which interpretation we adopt. If the pubilc treaty was a mere blind, no condemnation of Delcassé's policy can be too severe. If the intention to respect the political status of Morocco was sincere, we may confine ourselves to an emphatic disapproval of a transaction which lent itself so readily to misinterpretation. As a matter of fact, Delcassé's handling of the Morocco problem has found few whole-hearted champions except André Mévil, who sharply attacks the Premier Rouvier for his failure to support the policy of his colleague. " It was the initial mistake of not consulting the German Foreign Office," writes Mr. Evans Lewin in his valuable work ' The Germans in Africa,' " that led to the unfortunate crisis. Germany was completely ignored. France made a huge diplomatic blunder." The secret treaty, he adds, gave Germany an excuse for action. A similar verdict comes from Sir Thomas Barclay, a life-long friend of France. " That the *entente* was perverted by being made to appear anti-German is beyond question." Baron d'Estournelles de Constant condemned the secret clauses as " a double game," and statemen so generally opposed to each other as Ribot and Jaurès denounced the contradiction between public professions and private aims.

The invitation to a Conference was a direct challenge to Delcassé, and he naturally advised its rejection. But, as his policy had outpaced the defences of his country, he found himself alone in the Ministry and was forced to resign.* Some weeks later, in an interview in the *Gaulois*, he declared that in the event of war England would be with France, and added that Germany would not dare to face her fleet. A little later an article in the *Matin* stated that at the decisive

* In his Histoire diplomatique de l'Europe, 1879–1916, vol. 2, ch. i., Debidour contends that Rouvier desired to be rid of his colleague, in whom he scented a rival for the Premiership.

Cabinet meeting he had informed his colleagues of England's promise, in the event of war, to seize the Kiel Canal and land 100,000 men in Schleswig-Holstein. " I learned at the time of the crisis from a sure and direct source," wrote Jaurès in *l'Humanité* on October 12, " everything that Delcassé said to his colleagues of the intervention offered by England. I have this moment learned that she wished to make a written treaty to support us against Germany, not only by the mobilization of her fleet but by the disembarkation of 100,000 men." Four years later André Mévil, a personal friend of Delcassé, confirmed the story of a promise. At the end of May, 1905, he declares, the attitude of Germany was such as to compel France and England to take counsel together, and England promised armed assistance if France were attacked. He adds that England was ready to sign a definite undertaking, and that Lord Lansdowne informed the German ambassador in London that in the event of war France would not stand alone. That some promise of support was made is beyond doubt. Is there any reason why its nature and scope should not now be revealed by the British Government ?

Though French opinion generally approved the decision of the Rouvier Ministry to avoid the probability of war by accepting the invitation to a Conference, the crisis had created a disagreeable sense of impotence in face of German threats, and increased sums were voted for national defence. Both domestic and foreign observers agree in dating the birth of " New France " from the Kaiser's visit to Tangier. The termination of the Russo-Japanese war in August, by permitting her ally to resume her part in European politics, encouraged the self-confidence of the Republic, and the resolution of her ministers was further strengthened by the British assurance of support in a defensive war. To understand the deeper causes of this momentous departure in the history of British policy we must now turn to the story of Anglo-German relations.

III. ANGLO-GERMAN RELATIONS BEFORE 1906.

THE unification of Germany had been watched in England with sympathy if not with the enthusiasm inspired by Italy, and a royal marriage had increased the friendly interest with which the peoples regarded one another. No foreign potentate was so popular in England as " Frederick the Noble," and nowhere was the sympathy with his sufferings more pronounced. The cession of Heligoland in 1890 proclaimed to the world Lord Salisbury's confidence in the permanence of cordial relations, and the adjustment of territorial claims in Africa proceeded without the friction which marked the colonial expansion of France. Caprivi shewed himself openly Anglophil. In this peaceful atmosphere the Kaiser's telegram of congratulation to President Kruger on his repulse of the Jameson Raid exploded like a bomb. Though popularly regarded at the time as the personal act of an excitable ruler, the Foreign Secretary, Marschall von Bieberstein, told Sir Valentine Chirol on the following day that it was not a mere impulse of his master but " a State action." The Kaiser was surprised at the flaming indignation that it provoked, and Prince Henry has declared that his brother expressed his regrets to his relations at Windsor.

The Kruger telegram, however, was not the only sign that William II. had discarded the policy as well as rejected the tutelage of his old master. Bismarck had devoted the closing years of his dictatorship to

maintaining Germany's commanding position by securing the continued isolation of France. He effected
his purpose by an alliance with Austria and Italy,
by encouraging British and French colonial rivalry,
and by giving Russia a free hand in Turkey and the
Balkans. In a famous phrase he had declared that
his country was "satiated," and he only planted the
German flag in Africa in response to the pressure of
commercial interests. This cautious and conservative
policy was rejected by the young Emperor, who in
loyalty to his Austrian ally refused to renew the secret
"reinsurance treaty" with Russia, and who entered
into fearless competition for political influence and
economic concessions throughout the wide expanse
of the Turkish Empire. While Bismarck's triumphs
were won on the European chessboard, his successor
realized to the full the opportunities and requirements
of World-Policy. He learned the lessons of sea-power
from Mahan, and appealed for a fleet in the famous
words, " Our future lies on the water." No important
step in international policy, he declared, ought to be
taken without Germany being consulted. It was this
spirit which prompted the Kruger telegram, the occupation of Kiao-Chou, the pilgrimage to Jerusalem, the
invitation to the Mohammedans throughout the world
to look to him as their protector, the negotiations for
the Bagdad railway, and the creation of a mighty
fleet. It was a policy of glittering prizes and formidable risks, as *Weltpolitik* has always been.

In its early stages the new course created little if
any apprehension. The Kruger telegram was neither
forgotten nor forgiven ; but, as no further provocations
followed, the ruffled waters grew calm. Germany
consented, while France and Russia declined, to allow
the payment of the cost of the Dongola expedition

from the resources of the Debt. In 1898 Chamberlain, doubtless at the instigation of Rhodes, began negotiations with reference to the possible liquidation of the Portuguese colonies. The scheme has never been officially divulged ; but it appears that Mozambique was to be divided, the district north of the Zambesi falling to Germany, the south to Great Britain. As Germany's share was the least valuable, southern Angola was also adjudged to her. Though an agreement was reached no treaty was signed, partly, it is said, owing to Lord Salisbury's disapproval. But in the spring of 1899 Rhodes visited Berlin, and arranged for the continuation of the Cape to Cairo railway and telegraph through German East Africa.

In his Mansion House speech a month after the outbreak of the Boer war Lord Salisbury mentioned our cordial relations with Germany, and declared emphatically that they were all that could be desired. In the same month the Kaiser visited his grandmother, and Theodor Wolff relates that Bülow appealed to Chamberlain to join the Triple Alliance. Be that as it may, Chamberlain proceeded in his historic speech at Leicester to advocate a new Triple Alliance of Great Britain, the United States and Germany. That the plan was coldly received in the three countries concerned failed to impair the cordial relations of London and Berlin. According to *The Daily Telegraph* interview of 1908 the Kaiser received a letter from Queen Victoria written under the sorrowful emotions of the Black Week, and forwarded with his reply a plan of campaign drawn up by himself and revised by the General Staff. When invited by France and Russia to intervene, he declared in the same interview, he telegraphed to Windsor the terms of his refusal. When Kruger, crowned with roses at Paris, set out towards

Berlin, he was informed that the Kaiser would refuse him an audience. In October the two Governments signed a treaty to secure their commercial interests in China. In October, 1901, as we have recently learned from Sir Valentine Chirol,* the German Government initiated informal conversations with a view to an alliance guaranteeing the possession of the two Powers in every continent except Asia, where Germany desired to avoid a collision with Russia. The Foreign Editor of *The Times* was invited to Berlin, where Bülow spoke earnestly to him of his desire for a treaty of mutual defence.

This proposal registers the high-water mark of Anglo-German official intimacy, and its rejection, on the ground that it would fatally estrange us from France, marks the beginning of the ebb-tide. The German people, like the French, had loudly condemned the Boer war from the first, and the action of our fleet in stopping the Bundesrath and three other vessels off the east coast of Africa on the unfounded suspicion of contraband had created passionate resentment throughout the Fatherland, which was only partially mollified by an apology from the British Government. At the moment when the German proposal of mutual guarantees was rejected, a new explosion of popular feeling occurred. In rebuking the attacks of the German press on the conduct of the British army Chamberlain made a disparaging reference to the behaviour of German troops in 1870. Bülow retorted in the Reichstag that he was biting granite, and Chamberlain rejoined that he had nothing to withdraw. These oratorical fireworks, employing the first un-friendly words used by men of high official position, were received with applause by their respective com-patriots. A new era had begun.

* *Quarterly Review*, October, 1914.

The Kaiser had employed the excitement created by the stoppage of the Bundesrath to secure acceptance of an opulent programme of ship-building. Before he came to the throne he had recognised the importance of Heligoland, without which, in the words of Reventlow, a strong navy would have been impossible. British anger at the Kruger telegram, declares the same historian, converted Germany to the idea of a fleet ; and in 1897 a small programme of construction to be carried out by 1904 had been approved. But public feeling was not thoroughly aroused till the Spanish-American conflict and still more the Boer war demonstrated once again the importance of sea-power in the acquisition and maintenance of empire. The law of 1900 authorized the creation of a large fleet of powerful ships to be completed by 1917. The celebrated preamble defined its aim as the construction of a fleet so formidable that no other Power could attack it without risk. Thus began the naval rivalry which was to poison the relations of the two countries and threaten the peace of the world, and which finally issued in the clash of arms,

On the restoration of peace in South Africa it seemed as if something of the old friendliness might be restored, and the Kaiser declined to receive the Boer generals unless they were presented by the British Ambassador. But the fairer prospects were blighted once again. Germany had obtained a concession from the Sultan to construct a railway through Asia Minor to Bagdad and the Persian Gulf ; but the enterprise was too costly for a single Power. During his visit to England in 1903 the Kaiser invited his hosts to help to finance the great undertaking. The Balfour Ministry seemed to favour the suggestion ; but an outcry arose in a section of the press, and the invitation was declined.

The refusal was widely regarded in Germany as a piece of gratuitous unfriendliness. A still more unfavourable incident occurred in the early days of 1905. Long before England began to suspect the designs of the German fleet, fleetless Germany had felt alarm at the irresistible strength of the British navy ; and her apprehensions were strengthened by indiscretions in the English press. In 1897 an article in *The Saturday Review* contended that if Germany could be swept away to-morrow, every Englishman would be the richer. The mischievous nonsense attracted no attention in England, for the journal had passed its zenith ; but it was widely quoted abroad, and, like its successors, it has figured in every German indictment of British policy. In 1904 an article in *The Army and Navy Gazette*, suggesting that Great Britain should forbid any further increase of the German fleet, was accepted in Germany as the voice of the Admiralty. In 1905 a still more threatening note was struck by a member of the Ministry. In explaining to his constituents the object and results of the Fisher policy of concentrating the main force of the fleet in home waters, which Reventlow has described as " one of the epoch-making events of European history," Mr. Arthur Lee, Civil Lord of the Admiralty, was reported as saying that in certain eventualities it would be possible to strike the first blow before the inhabitants of the enemy country knew that war was declared. The speaker in vain complained that he had been incorrectly reported, and large sections of the German people now began to believe that their country was threatened by a sudden attack. The construction of the first Dreadnought intensified the feeling of danger and impotence, and the navy programme of 1900 was accordingly enlarged in 1906 by the addition of six

large cruisers. " If we had not replied to the Dreadnought," comments Reventlow, " the fear of the German
fleet would have ended and 'good relations' would
easily have been reached ; but we should have lived
under English patronage in all sea and oversea questions. It would have been a second Fashoda." The
naval rivalry herewith entered on a new and more
dangerous stage. Tirpitz was planted firmly in the
saddle, and the ambitions of certain influential schools
of thought became at once more menacing and more
articulate.

IV. THE CONFERENCE OF ALGECIRAS.

WE may now return to the moment when, on the eve
of the conference at Algeciras, a Liberal Ministry was
formed by Campbell-Bannerman. The French Government at once asked the new Foreign Minister, Sir
Edward Grey, whether help would be forthcoming
in a war with Germany arising out of the problem of
Morocco. This incident was only revealed many years
later when on August 3, 1914, the Foreign Minister
proceeded to unveil the history of British obligations,
omitting, curiously enough, all reference to the similar
action apparently taken only a few months earlier
by his predecessor in office. " When a General Election
was in progress and Ministers were scattered over the
country, I was asked the question whether, if that
crisis developed into war between France and Germany,
we would give armed support. I said then that I could
promise nothing to any foreign Power unless it was
subsequently to receive the whole-hearted support
of public opinion here if the occasion arose. I said,
in my opinion, if war was forced upon France
on the question of Morocco—a question which had

just been the subject of agreement, an agreement exceedingly popular on both sides—that if out of that agreement war was forced on France, in my view public opinion in this country would have rallied to the material support of France. I gave no promise, but I expressed that opinion during the crisis to the French Ambassador and the German Ambassador. I made no promise and I used no threats. That position was accepted by the French Government; but they said to me at the time, and I think very reasonably, ' If you think it possible that the public opinion of Great Britain might, should a sudden crisis arise, justify you in giving to France the armed support which you cannot promise in advance, you will not be able to give that support, even if you wish it, when the time comes, unless some conversations have already taken place between naval and military experts.' There was force in that. I agreed to it, and authorized those conversations to take place, but on the distinct understanding that nothing which passed between military or naval experts should bind either Government or restrict in any way their freedom to make a decision as to whether or not they would give that support when the time arose. I had to take the responsibility of doing that without the Cabinet. It could not be summoned. An answer had to be given. I consulted Sir Henry Campbell-Bannerman, the Prime Minister; I consulted Lord Haldane, who was then Secretary of State for War; and the present Prime Minister (Mr. Asquith), who was then Chancellor of the Exchequer. That was the most I could do, and they authorized that on the distinct understanding that it left the hands of the Government free whenever the crisis arose. The fact that conversations between military and naval experts took place was later on—

I think much later on, because that crisis passed and
the thing ceased to be of importance—but later on it
was brought to the knowledge of the Cabinet."

This renewal of a confidential assurance of armed
support confirmed the new departure in British policy.
M. Tardieu's summary verdict, " C'est la crainte de
l'Allemagne qui avait fait l'entente cordiale," is in-
correct as far as Great Britain is concerned ; for the
British negotiators of the treaty of 1904 were moved
neither by fear of nor hostility towards Germany.
Their object was to bury the controversies of a generation, not to join one of the rival European groups.
But the events of 1905 were too much for them.
Conversations began to take place not only with French
experts but, as we learned after the German occupation
of Brussels, with Belgians. The most significant
result of these conversations was to be the virtual
withdrawal of the French fleet from the North and
West coasts of France, and the diminution of British
naval strength in the Mediterranean. On the one
side obligations, however indefinite, were incurred,
and on the other expectations, however nebulous,
were encouraged. It was a policy of transition in a
period of racing change ; but it corresponded pretty
closely to the feelings of the governing classes of Great
Britain. While France was so new a friend and Germany so new a danger, a policy of limited liability
might well appear the safest path.

When the Conference of the signatories of the Treaty
of Madrid met at Algeciras in January, 1906, the Powers
at once fell into two groups.* France, stoutly backed
by Russia and Great Britain, fought for special privi-
leges for herself and Spain, while Germany championed

---

* The Conference is fully described from the French standpoint by
Tardieu, La Conférence d'Algésiras.

the policy of international responsibility dictated by her interests. Austria, in the words of the Kaiser, played the part of a brilliant second in the duel. Italy, on the other hand, rendered as little support to her ally as she dared ; for she had obtained the consent of France to her ultimate absorption of Tripoli, facilitating in return the execution of French designs in Morocco. The chief difficulty was the control of the police in the coast towns. While Germany and Austria wished the Sultan to select the officers where he liked, or, if a limitation was imposed, from the small States alone, the other Powers advocated the claims of France and Spain. Finally Austria suggested and carried the compromise, which virtually conceded the French demand, that a limited number of French and Spanish officers should serve under a Swiss Inspector-General. Though the integrity of Morocco was recognized once again, the condition of unstable equilibrium remained. France was compelled by disturbances to occupy Udja on the Algerian frontier, and Casablanca and the Shawia district on the Atlantic coast ; and it was soon obvious that her troops had come to stay. In 1908 a dangerous quarrel arising out of the arrest of German deserters at Casablanca was settled by the Hague Tribunal, and in 1909 Germany recognized the special political interests of France in return for a pledge of commercial co-operation. The final stage of the controversy will claim our attention at a later period.

V. THE ENTENTE WITH RUSSIA.

DURING the Conference of Algeciras the Anglo-French *entente,* to adopt the expressive phrase of Tardieu, passed from the static to the dynamic stage. But it could never be water-tight while Great Britain and

Russia scowled at one another, and it was to the termination of the ancient feud that the statesmen of both countries now turned their attention. The Tsar had begun to discuss the questions at issue with Sir Charles Hardinge, the British Ambassador at St. Petersburg, in 1905, and the common support of France throughout the heated discussions at Algeciras, where Great Britain was represented by Sir Arthur Nicolson, her ambassador to Russia, had brought the Chancelleries nearer together. In the same year the City of London, after a long interval, took part in an Anglo-French loan. Sir Edward Grey, assisted by the India Office, devoted his whole strength to the task, and after long negotiations an agreement was signed in August, 1907. While the Anglo-French treaty had clasped the whole world in its embrace, the new compact was confined to the Middle East. When Lord Salisbury buried our Turkophil policy beneath the epitaph, " We put our money on the wrong horse," the oldest source of friction was happily removed, and only the Indian problem now remained. Accordingly the treaty dealt with Thibet, Afghanistan and Persia, the three States which from their geographical position had proved and might prove again the occasion of trouble between the two great Empires.

British statesmen had felt growing apprehension as to Russian intrigues in the thinly-populated and unwarlike theocracy of Thibet, and in 1904 Lord Curzon persuaded the Balfour Ministry to send an armed mission to Lhassa. The sacred city was entered after slight resistance, the Dalai Lama fled, and a treaty was signed by Colonel Younghusband with his successor, providing for a Resident in Lhassa, facilities for trade, and the retention of the Chumbi valley while an indemnity was paid by instalments. The treaty, how-

ever, was substantially modified by the Home Government, which had no desire to intervene in Thibetan
affairs ; and so strictly was the principle of neutraliza-
tion interpreted that even scientific explorers were
forbidden to enter the country.   When the two Powers
began to negotiate it was thus easy to reach agreement.
The signatories pledged themselves to respect Thibetan
integrity, to abstain from all interference in internal
affairs, to seek no economic concessions, to send no
representatives to Lhassa, and to deal with the State
exclusively through the government of its suzerain,
China. In Afghanistan, a name recalling a long and
dangerous rivalry, Russia made an important concession. Great Britain declared that she had no intention of altering the political status of the country,
and bound herself to occupy no territory, to use her
influence in a peaceful way, to abstain from measures
threatening to Russia, and to avoid interference so
long as the Amir fulfilled his obligations. Russia,
for her part, recognising that Afghanistan lay outside
her sphere of influence, undertook to send no agents
into the country and to employ the British Government
as a medium for all political communications. That
the consent of the Amir to this arrangement has never
been obtained is of slight importance.

Russia's deference to British claims in Afghanistan
was met by the British concession to Russian claims
in Persia, as Egypt and Morocco had been balanced
against one another. It was this section of the treaty
which presented the greatest difficulties and possessed
by far the greatest importance. Russia had long
exerted a predominant influence in the north, where
the frontier marched with her own. Great Britain, again,
which had cleared the Persian Gulf of pirates and had
policed it for a century, had in recent years formally

announced that she would allow no other Power to establish a naval base. In the negotiations which now took place our paramount concern was to guard the approaches to India by sea and land. An agreement was finally reached which, while recognizing the integrity and independence of Persia, mapped out spheres of influence. The Russian Foreign Minister, Izvolsky, relates Dr. Dillon, proposed to divide the whole country between the two Powers ; but Great Britain insisted on the creation of a buffer territory, and the Indian Government advised against the assignment of a larger territory than it could defend. The Russian sphere embraced the north and centre, which included the richest and most populous districts and the three large cities of Tabriz, Teheran and Ispahan. The British sphere was confined to the south and east, embracing the coastal districts of the Gulf and the Indian Ocean and stretching away to the frontiers of Beluchistan. Each Power undertook to seek no political or commercial concession in the other's sphere. The remaining territory separating the two spheres of influence was recognized as a neutral zone, in which both Powers might obtain concessions. In addition to the treaty Russia recognized our special interest in the Persian Gulf as set forth in a despatch from Sir Edward Grey to the British Ambassador in St. Petersburg. The delimitation of the zones was sharply attacked by Lord Curzon, Earl Percy, and other Imperialist critics as unduly favourable to Russia. The Government replied that the treaty must be judged as a whole, that the safety of India was fully secured, and that the removal of dangerous differences was well worth the price that it had cost.

The reconciliation of ancient foes was followed, as had been the case with France, by diplomatic co-operation in various fields. The Anglo-French Entente speedily developed into the Triple Entente, which confronted the Triple Alliance on the European chessboard. Though Great Britain was not allied to any Power except Japan and Portugal, and in theory retained perfect liberty of action, she had now half unwittingly, but none the less definitely, thrown in her lot with France and Russia. It was this novel system of attachments which was to govern our policy in the coming years and to determine its course in Persia, the Balkans, and Morocco.

VI. PERSIA.

THE Treaty of 1907 was criticized by a section of British opinion on the ground that it threatened the independence of Persia, which had recently made a series of gallant efforts to set her house in order. When Muzaffer-ed-din, who ascended the throne in 1890, had squandered the scanty resources of his people in costly journeys to Europe, he was driven to Russian loans. The general mortgaging of the country to her mighty northern neighbour was watched with jealousy by Great Britain and with indignation by self-respecting Persians. In 1906 an explosion of popular feeling occurred, and thousands of citizens took refuge in the grounds of the British Legation at Teheran. The Shah was forced to grant a Constitution, and a national assembly met in the autumn. In the following year the Shah died and was succeeded by his son, Mohammed Ali, whose initial hostility to the Constitution was intensified by the reduction of his Civil List, and who was only prevented from executing his Ministers by the intervention of the British Chargé d'affaires. In 1908, after an attempt on his life, he fled to the Summer Palace outside the capital, whence he carried out a *coup d'état* with the aid of the "Cossack Brigade," which for many years had been under the command of Russian officers. The Parliament House was bombarded, Colonel Liakhoff was appointed Military Governor of the capital, and the reformers fled for their lives. The Constitutionalists held out in Tabriz during the winter, closely invested by the Shah's forces. When the fall of the city became imminent, Russian troops crossed the frontier to its relief. The Baktiaris, a fighting tribe of the south, now marched to Teheran and compelled the Shah to abdicate. His youthful heir was placed on the throne under a Regency, the Mejliss was recalled and the work of reform resumed.

The task was difficult, the actors were inexperienced, and the Treasury was empty. Accordingly in 1911, Mr. Shuster, an American of high character and ability, selected by President Taft, was invited to assume control of the finances and quickly gained the affectionate confidence of earnest reformers. For a moment it seemed as if a new day might dawn for Persia. But Mr. Shuster made a tactical mistake which, however natural and honourable, was to prove fatal to himself and to the cause of national regeneration which he was eager to serve. " I was early offered the plain choice," he writes, " between serving the Persian people and only appearing to do so, while actually serving foreign interests bent on Persia's national destruction." Considering himself the servant of the Government by which he was appointed and paid and responsible to no other authority, he omitted to call at the British and Russian embassies. The Anglo-Russian Treaty recognized Persia as an independent State, and the economic claims of the signatories in the spheres of influence carried with them no political rights. Mr. Shuster's interpretation was confirmed by an emphatic *communiqué* from the British Legation at Teheran to the Persian Government when the Treaty was signed, of which the following extract gives some idea : " Information has reached me that the report is rife in Persia that the result of the agreement between England and Russia will be the intervention of these two Powers in Persia, and the partition of Persia between them. The object of the two Powers in making this agreement is not in any way to attack, but rather to assure for ever the independence of Persia. Not only do they not wish to have at hand any excuse for intervention, but their object in these friendly negotiations was not to allow one another to intervene on the pretext of safeguarding their interests. The two Powers hope that in the future Persia will be for ever delivered from the fear of foreign intervention, and will thus be perfectly free to manage her own affairs in her own way." Curiously enough, this official document, to which so much weight was naturally attached by the Persian constitutionalists, remained for years unknown to Sir Edward Grey. On the other hand, a series of Russian interventions in questions of administration shewed that she interpreted her rights in a widely different manner.

Under these circumstances collisions were inevitable. For instance, when Mr. Shuster chose Major Stokes, a British officer who spoke Persian, as commander of the gendarmerie to secure the collection of the taxes, the appointment was vetoed from St. Petersburg on the ground that no Englishman might exercise authority in the Russian sphere. After eight months of uphill but fruitful effort, continually interrupted by friction with Russia, the Treasurer was expelled by a Russian ultimatum, which was approved by Sir Edward Grey.

"Mr. Shuster," writes Prof. Murray in his defence of Anglo-Russian policy, " was a man of irreproachable integrity and indomitable resolution ; but ironic fate had decreed that one small wrong-headedness should wreck everything. He happened to be both a very headstrong man and a prejudiced Russophobe. He acted like the head of an independent kingdom, intolerant of control within and impatient of diplomatic courtesies without. I can hardly understand how any one could have expected Russian authorities to submit to Mr. Shuster much longer." The " prejudiced Russophobe " has told the poignant story in ' The Strangling of Persia,' from which the reader can form his own impressions of his conduct and personality. It is unnecessary to idealize a decaying empire or to regard all or even the majority of the constitutionalists as disinterested patriots in order to regret the first-fruits of the Anglo-Russian *entente*. It is difficult to resist the impression that his mission was doomed from the start, and that Russia had no desire for a prosperous and self-respecting State which might resist the extension of her influence. St. Petersburg, declares Dr. Dillon, an apologist of the Russian Government, was loyal to the Treaty of 1907, but her agents were not. The distinction, if it existed, was no consolation to Persian patriots. Mr. Shuster, whatever his faults, was the best friend that modern Persia has had, and with his expulsion the country relapsed into hopeless anarchy.

Sir Edward Grey repeatedly explained and defended his Persian policy in Parliament. Descriptions of the lamentable condition of the country were met by the reply that things would have been even worse had not the Treaty been signed. Complaints of Russia's interference were countered by the argument that the spirit of the agreement demanded that within her sphere of interest she should have a free hand. In plain English, support of Russian claims in Persia was the price of the treaty of 1907, as support of French claims in Morocco was the price of the treaty of 1904. If those claims went further than was expected or approved, the European situation rendered it difficult if not impossible to challenge them without danger.

VII. The Bosnian Crisis.

A few months after the dual Alliance had expanded into the Triple Entente, the waters of European diplomacy were once more churned into foam. In February, 1908, the world was startled by an announcement that Count Aehrenthal had obtained permission from the Sultan to make a survey for the construction of a railway through the Sanjak of Novibazar, which Austria had garrisoned since the Treaty of Berlin. To ask such a favour at a time when the only hope of Macedonian reform lay in steady pressure from the Powers appeared something like treason to the Concert. Moreover, it opened the door to other ambitions, and Serbia immediately put forward a demand, supported by Russia, for a railway to the Adriatic. The quarrel of Austria and Russia added importance to the visit of King Edward in June to the Czar at Reval, the first ever paid to Russia by a British sovereign, which was universally regarded as a demonstration of the new Anglo-Russian solidarity. Early in the year Sir Edward Grey, who had inherited Lord Lansdowne's active sympathy for the Christian victims of Ottoman misrule, foreshadowed the appointment of a Christian Governor of Macedonia, as the steps hitherto taken by the Powers had failed to terminate the anarchy of that unhappy province. The problem was discussed

at Reval, and it was in part the fear of foreign intervention that precipitated the rebellion of the Young Turks. The overthrow of Abdul-Hamid and the restoration of the constitution of 1876 were welcomed throughout Western Europe; and the international machinery of the Murzsteg programme and the Financial Commission was scrapped in the belief that Turkey would now reform herself.

The bright prospects of reform and racial reconciliation faded away when Bulgaria threw off the suzerainty of Turkey, and Austria announced the annexation of Bosnia and Herzegovina, at the same time renouncing her right to the military occupation of Novibazar.* In a moment the whole of the Near East was in a ferment. Serbia demanded compensation for the destruction of her hopes of union with Bosnia and Herzegovina, while Montenegro pressed for the removal of the fetters on her seaboard. Lord Redesdale, who was staying at Balmoral when the news arrived, has described in his Memoirs the anger of King Edward, who had discussed the Balkan situation with Francis Joseph and Aehrenthal only two months before. Sir Edward Grey at once announced that any modification of the Treaty of Berlin must be approved by another European Congress, just as Russia's repudiation of the Black Sea clauses of the Treaty of Paris was discussed and condoned in 1871. Russia and France supported the demand; but as Bulgaria and Austria compounded for their sins by a cash indemnity the danger of war with Turkey was thus removed, and Aehrenthal opposed an unyielding front to the claims of Serbia.

* See the valuable chapter on Foreign Policy in Steed, The Hapsburg Monarchy. A full account of the whole transaction from the Austrian point of view is given in Sosnosky's important work, Die Balkanpolitik Oesterreich-Ungarns seit 1866, vol. ii., chapter 5.

Achrenthal had informed Izvolsky academically in
the summer that Austria would some day annex the
provinces, and asked his opinion on the project. Izvolsky replied that in his opinion it would not be regarded
as a *casus belli*, but that compensation would be demanded, such as the opening of the Straits to Russian
war ships and the revision of the articles of the Treaty
of Berlin affecting Bulgaria, Serbia, Montenegro, and
Novibazar. As Achrenthal promised to inform his
visitor if and when annexation was definitely determined,
the speedy and secret execution of the plan came as
a shock to St. Petersburg.* As the winter advanced
excitement steadily grew. The Serbian Crown Prince
George talked wildly of war with Austria ; but the
tension was ended in March, 1909, by a warning from
the Kaiser to the Tsar that if Russian encouragement
of Serbian ambitions were to lead to a collision with
Austria, Germany would support her ally with all her
forces. Russia was unready for war, the opposition
instantly collapsed, and the annexation was unconditionally recognized. Achrenthal had played a bold
game and won ; but the price of his victory was the
aggrieved antagonism of Russia. On visiting the
King of Italy shortly after the Tsar ostentatiously
avoided passing through Austrian territory. He was
to bury his feud with the Kaiser at Potsdam in the
following year, Germany giving Russia a free hand
in Persia, and Russia withdrawing her opposition to
the Bagdad railway. But he never forgave Francis
Joseph, and the humiliation of 1909 rankled into one
of the primary causes of the war of 1914.

The diplomatic support given by Great Britain to
Russia throughout the crisis was a further demonstration
of the solidarity of the Triple Entente. Sir Charles

---

* Trubetzkoi, ' Russland als Grossmacht,' 110-114 and 152-3,

Dilke bluntly told the Foreign Secretary that he was
making too much fuss about the formal incorporation
of provinces which for all practical purposes had
belonged to the Hapsburg Empire for a generation.
Moreover, Austria had at the time received permission
from Great Britain, Germany and Russia to annex the
provinces at once and had only refrained from doing
so at the wish of Andrassy, who voluntarily acknowledged the provisional character of the occupation.*
Sir Edward firmly replied that the principle of sacredness
of public law was at stake. But his contention that
changes in the public law of Europe must be made
or at least ratified by international action was precisely
the argument on which a few years earlier Germany
had based her invitation to the signatories of the Treaty
of Madrid to take part in a conference at Algeciras.
In a world of alliances and *ententes* what is sauce for
the goose is not always sauce for the gander.

VIII. The Problem of Armaments.

The growing intimacy of Great Britain with France
and Russia ran parallel with her increasing estrange-
ment from Germany. European politics, indeed, had
now begun to revolve in a vicious circle. The alarming
increase of the German navy and the vaulting ambitions
of the Pan-Germans drove Great Britain into ever
closer intimacy with France and Russia, while the
growing solidarity of the Triple Entente stimulated
the demand in Germany for the strengthening of her
national defences. Lord Lansdowne and Sir Edward
Grey had repeatedly declared that their policy of
ententes had no " point " directed against any other

* A similar criticism is directed by Prince Troubetzkoi against
Izvolsky, ' Russland als Grossmacht,' 113-114. England's attitude is,
of course, sharply condemned by Sosnosky, II, 156-162.

Power ; but after Algeciras this disclaimer was never accepted in Germany, where the legend arose that King Edward was ceaselessly plotting to encircle and " hem in " the Fatherland. That the delusion was not confined to Germans is proved by the remarkable dispatches of Belgian diplomats discovered and published in 1914 after the German occupation of Brussels. His real attitude has been thus defined by Lord Esher. " He was not only a peace-maker but a peace-lover. He had been reared in the belief that Europe and the world would be all the better for the unification of Germany under Prussian leadership. The absurd press campaigns in the two countries saddened and annoyed him. No one could be long in his vicinity without discovering that he liked Germany and the German people. No one could have watched the King and the Kaiser together without noticing that the two men, in spite of difference of temperament and divergence of ideals, bore a curious likeness to each other, that blood is thicker than water, and that not only mutual respect but real admiration underlay their intercourse." His political innocence is corroborated by Sir Sidney Lee's categorical assurance that " he had no conception of any re-adjustment of European power." The tension, however, was now reaching danger-point, and it became the main preoccupation of British statesmen to heal the running sore. They approached the problem, however, with two fundamental reservations which, in the light of subsequent events, may well appear to have rendered success impossible. Those essential conditions were the maintenance of a supreme navy and unswerving fidelity to the Triple Entente.

However innocent may have been the designs of the German Government in the creation of a powerful navy, and however sincere the official and unofficial assurances of the Kaiser and his Ministers as to its non-aggressive character, it could not fail to appear as a threat to a country which depended for its security and its food entirely on the invincibility of its fleet. No British statesman contested the right of Germany to follow the example of the Great Powers of Europe, of Japan and of the United States, or maintained that such an act was in itself a proof of evil resolutions ; but unless we could be satisfied that the strongest military Power in the world had no intention of challenging the foundations of our national existence, suspicions were inevitable and steps had to be taken to strengthen ourselves against a possible menace. " I never advocated an unlimited naval policy," declares Prince Bülow ; but unfortunately for herself and for the peace of the world, Germany's face has always been set like flint against all plans of limitation. Prince Bülow has explained his policy in the frankest terms.* " In 1897 we lay at England's mercy like so much butter before the knife. For the sake of our interests, as well as our honour and dignity, we were obliged to see that we won for our international policy the same independence that we had secured for our European policy. The fleet that we have built since 1897, though far inferior to England's, enables us to support our interests everywhere with all the weight of our reputation as a Great Power." " To have renounced our naval policy in order to please England," he adds in a passage written after the outbreak of war,† " would have been tantamount to declaring the bankruptcy of Germany as a rising World Power." Compelled to choose between a great navy and the friendship of the British Empire, the Kaiser, Bülow, and Tirpitz deliberately chose the former.

---

* In Imperial Germany, 1st edition.
† Edition of 1916.

The German refusal to discuss the burden of armaments had rendered the first Hague Conference of 1899
almost futile. Again, when in July, 1906, the Campbell-
Bannerman Ministry gave a lead to the Powers invited
to the second Conference by reducing its programme
of battle-ships, destroyers, and submarines, the Emperor
William informed Sir Frank Lascelles that if the question of armaments was to be brought up at the Hague
he must decline to be represented. When King Edward
visited Cronberg in the summer, the Kaiser remarked
to Sir Charles Hardinge that the approaching Conference
was great nonsense. That his attitude was not dictated
by hostility to England was shewn by his permission
to Lord Haldane, whom he had invited to attend the
autumn manœuvres, to make a detailed study of the
work of the German War Office.* In the spring of
1907 the British Premier returned to the charge in an
article in *The Nation*, announcing that the Government,
which had made unconditional reductions in its programme of 1906, was now prepared to go further if
other Powers would follow suit. At the same time
our desire that the reduction of armaments should be
considered at the Hague was officially communicated
to the seven chief naval Powers. Prince Bülow replied in the Reichstag that Germany could not take
part in the discussion, which she regarded as unpractical
if not dangerous. " When England had invented
the Dreadnought," sneers Reventlow, " she wished
to make use of the Conference to arrest competition.
Campbell-Bannerman may have been sincere, but
his proposal would have left Germany in leading-
strings." Under these circumstances Sir Edward Fry
was instructed to state at the Conference that his
Government was ready to exchange its naval estimates

* Begbie, 'The Vindication of Great Britain,' ch. 3.

in advance with any other Power, in the hope that a reduction might thus be secured. The financial aspect of the naval rivalry was, of course, important ; but our governing principle was the humane desire to remove the cause of the growing tension.

When the second Hague Conference was over the Kaiser paid a visit to Windsor in November, bringing with him his Foreign Minister and Minister for War. " It seems that some kind of verbal agreement was reached during those days of festivity concerning the Bagdad railway," writes Mr. Begbie in a chapter revised by Lord Haldane. " Apparently, Great Britain had expressed her willingness that the German Emperor should go ahead with his railway, provided that her own obvious interests were safeguarded, and that her partners in the Entente were consulted before any agreement was ratified. He was not averse from the proposition of a Conference between his country and the Entente Powers, but he would have preferred an agreement between England and Germany. I have good reasons for saying that King Edward was highly delighted by the result of the Windsor visit. For the first time since the beginning of strained relations a feeling of confidence seemed to exist between Germany and England. But the Emperor had counted without his Chancellor, whose suspicions of the Entente were confirmed by Great Britain's refusal to come into a conference without Russia and France." Thus the second attempt to reach an agreement on the Bagdad railway failed, this time owing not to British Ministers but to Prince Bülow.

During the summer of 1908 Edward VII. visited his nephew, accompanied by Sir Charles Hardinge, who was commissioned by the Foreign Secretary to propose an exchange of ideas on the navies between the two

Governments. The Kaiser expressed his good will towards England, but firmly refused to tolerate any such discussion with a foreign Power. In February, 1909, King Edward paid his first official visit to Berlin, and it seemed as if warmer airs were about to blow; but shortly after his return rumours were spread that Germany was secretly accelerating her naval programme, and the speeches of Mr. McKenna and Mr. Asquith in introducing very large estimates in March created something like a panic. Their fears were not realized, for the German Government was able to shew that no real acceleration was taking place; but the fever of suspicion began to burn fiercely in the blood of the British people. To obviate the repetition of such a shock Sir Edward Grey proposed that the naval attachés in Berlin and London should be allowed from time to time to see the actual stage of construction of the capital ships; but the proposal was declined by Germany.

At this time, in July, 1909, Bülow was succeeded by Bethmann-Hollweg, who immediately applied himself to the amelioration of Anglo-German relations. " During my term of office," writes the Prince, " I was convinced that a conflict between Germany and England would never come to pass : (1) if we built a fleet which could not be attacked without very grave risk ; (2) if we did not indulge in undue and unlimited ship-building ; (3) if we did not allow England to injure our reputation or our dignity ; (4) if we did nothing to make an irremediable breach between us and England ; (5) if we kept calm and cool, and neither affronted England nor ran after her." This policy was wholly negative, and the Prince resolutely refused to discuss the root of the difficulty. The story of his successor's endeavours has been told from official sources by Sir

Edward Cook in his pamphlet, published after the outbreak of war, ' How Britain strove for Peace.'

The new Chancellor informed the British Ambassador that he realized the naval question to be regarded by Great Britain as the chief obstacle to cordiality, and that he was ready to propose a naval arrangement. The discussion, he added, could only be useful as part of a general understanding based on a conviction that neither country had hostile designs against the other. The British Government replied that they would gladly consider any proposals for a general understanding consistent with existing obligations to other Powers. The Chancellor then stated that though the Navy Law could not be modified, he was willing to discuss retardation. Though the total number of vessels to be completed by 1918 would not be altered, the number of capital ships might be reduced in the earlier years and proportionately increased in the later. In return for this offer he asked for a signed agreement that neither country had any idea of aggression nor would attack the other, and that in the event of an attack made on either signatory by a third Power or group of Powers, the other should remain neutral. The British Government refused to bind itself to neutrality, apprehensive of the effect of such a pledge on the other members of the Entente. Without in any way doubting the personal good faith of the Chancellor, the British Government was haunted by visions of a European war which might leave Great Britain without a friend confronting a Power drunk with victory and ambition. Even had the naval offer been more substantial a similar reply would have been given.

Nearly a year later negotiations were resumed. In July, 1910, Mr. Asquith, speaking on the Naval Estimates, announced that the German Government had declined to modify its programme. The Chancellor replied that, though unable to accept reduction, he was still ready to discuss retardation. The British Government thereupon withdrew its earlier claim for a reduction of the programme and expressed itself ready to discuss retardation. The German programme should not be increased, and information on the progress of ship-building should be exchanged. On the question of political relations we were ready to assert that there was nothing directed against Germany in our obligations to other Powers, and that we had no hostile intentions. Negotiations continued through the winter ; but in May, 1911, the German offer of temporary retardation was withdrawn on the ground that the ship-building industry had to be supported by Government orders. The British Cabinet was considering its reply to the question what equivalent they would offer for a promise not to enlarge the programme, when the Kaiser informed the British Ambassador that he would never agree thus to tie his hands. Though the Chancellor was thus thrown over, the German Government declared itself ready to examine any proposals for a mutual reduction of expenditure which did not involve the modification of the Navy Law. The parallel discussions on political relationships seemed a trifle more hopeful. The Chancellor once more expressed his desire for a precise formula, while Sir Edward Grey pointed out that the agreements with France and Russia had not been made by a formula but by the removal of specific difficulties. Discussions were proceeding when they were violently interrupted by the Agadir crisis.

IX. AGADIR.

THE concluding article of the Treaty of Algeciras, which re-affirmed the independence of Morocco, ran as follows : " All existing treaties, conversations and arrangements between the signatory Powers and Morocco remain in force. It is, however, agreed that in case their provisions be found to conflict with those of the present Act, the stipulations of the latter shall prevail." Three years later France signed a joint Declaration with Germany professing herself " firmly attached to the maintenance of the independence and integrity of the Shereefian Empire." Germany recognized " the special political interests of France," while France undertook " not to obstruct German commercial and industrial interests." This economic partnership, however, led to endless friction ; for it was differently interpreted in Paris and Berlin. The exploitation of mines and the construction of public works were the subject of heated discussion ; but a still thornier problem was that of the railways, which might be classified as politics or economics according to taste. When at the end of 1910 the French military authorities in Morocco were contemplating the construction of two lines, the German Government demanded a share in the transaction. The French Ambassador reported the significance attached in Berlin to the question, and the German Ambassador in Paris asked for a speedy settlement. The Foreign Minister, Pichon, at once sketched out an agreement ; but in an evil moment he was replaced by Cruppi, whose delays exasperated Cambon. A final modification proposed from Paris was accepted at Berlin, and Cambon asked permission to sign. Cruppi's answer was that he must weigh its terms. While the railway treaty was thus suspended in the air, rumours of military action in Morocco reached

Berlin, and Kiderlen-Wächter remarked to Cambon that by successsive military operations France might be led into an occupation which would annul the Act of Algeciras. His words were scarcely spoken when an expedition to Fez, on the ground that the Sultan was unable to defend himself or the European residents against the insurgent tribes, was notified to the Powers. It was now too late to sign the railway agreement. "In four months," wrote M. Georges Bourdon,[*] "neither the good will of Germany, nor the representations of our ambassador, nor the pressure of circumstances which commanded us to conciliate dangerous critics just when we were about to need their approval, had succeeded in concluding an arrangement based on the Act of Algeciras and which would have formed the first instalment of the pact of 1909. Let us dare to say the truth—it is a pitiable story."

The news of the expedition to Fez caused intense irritation in Berlin, where the danger to Europeans was dismissed as a diplomatic fiction. "I cannot encourage you," remarked the Chancellor to Cambon; "I advise you to be cautious." "If you are once in Fez," said Kiderlen-Wächter, "you will not be able to leave; if the power of the Sultan needs French bayonets to support it, we shall consider that the Act of Algeciras is broken and we shall resume our liberty of action." The threats were unheeded at Paris, and in May the troops entered the Moroccan capital. A month later Cambon was instructed to offer Kiderlen-Wächter satisfaction, but to add that Germany must not expect any part of Morocco. But a momentous decision had already been taken. Ten days later the Panther, a small German gunboat, anchored in the open roadstead of Agadir, in southern Morocco, and was followed by a light cruiser.

_____

* 'L'Énigme Allemande,' ch. 1.

When the sensational news of the Panther's spring reached London, Sir Edward Grey, who had publicly approved the expedition to Fez, informed the German Ambassador that he took so serious a view of the matter that it must be discussed by a Cabinet. Next day (July 4), after the meeting, he explained the attitude of the Government. A new situation, he declared, had been created. Future developments might affect British interests more directly than hitherto, and therefore we could not recognize any new arrangements that might be concluded without us. A similar declaration was made shortly after by the Prime Minister in Parliament. On July 21, Sir Edward sent for the German Ambassador, expressed his surprise at receiving no communication from Berlin, and added that news from Paris of exorbitant German demands made him anxious. The same evening Mr. Lloyd George, speaking at the Mansion House, used the following words, which had been drawn up with the assistance of the Prime Minister and the Foreign Secretary, but without the knowledge of the Cabinet : " I am bound to say this ; that I believe it is essential in the higher interests not merely of this country but of the world, that Britain should at all hazards maintain her place and her prestige amongst the great Powers of the world. If a situation were to be forced on us in which peace could only be preserved by the surrender of the great and beneficent position Britain has won by centuries of heroism and achievements, by allowing Britain to be treated, where her interests were vitally affected, as if she were of no account in the Cabinet of Nations, then I say emphatically that peace at that price would be a humiliation intolerable for a great country like ours to endure."

The champions of Sir Edward contend that his conversation with Wolff-Metternich on July 4 demanded

an immediate reply from Berlin. " It was impossible,"
writes Prof. Murray, " that our Government should not
feel uneasy. There was known to be a strong war-party
in Germany. There was known to be a party in favour
of a very ambitious colonial policy. We had asked in
the most earnest way for a very simple assurance, and
had been met by stony silence." Meanwhile information
arrived from Paris that Germany was presenting impossible demands. To stop this dangerous game Great
Britain raised her voice ; and the Chancellor of the
Exchequer assured his friends that his speech had
prevented war. The critics of the Foreign Secretary, on
the other hand, reply that his conversation on July 4
was an announcement, not an interrogation ; that when
on July 12 the British Ambassador at Berlin mentioned
the rumour that his country was to be excluded from
conversations between Germany, France, and Spain
the Foreign Minister replied that there had never been
such an idea ; that the story of " impossible " demands
came not from the French Government, but from the
Paris office of *The Times*, which proved itself throughout
the crisis *plus royaliste que le roi ;* and that the Mansion
House speech, if made at all, should have been postponed
till the reply of the German Government to Sir Edward's
communication of July 21 had been received.

The response from Berlin was brought on July 24 ;
but it was now a reply not only to the conversation of
July· 21 but to the Mansion House speech as well. In
view of that threat the German Government refused to
allow Sir Edward to make public the pledge that Germany
had no territorial designs on Morocco, and Sir Edward
refused to give any public explanation of his colleague's
utterance. The two men stood on their dignity ; but
three days later they had a frank and amicable conversation, the Prime Minister made a conciliatory speech,

and the worst was over. An objective verdict on the action of the Foreign Secretary will only become possible when we learn the whole story of the successive demands and intentions of the German Government.* The German commercial interests in Morocco raised a loud outcry, and the Pan-Germans, who had rapidly grown in numbers, influence, and truculent audacity, had long demanded that part if not the whole of the country should be secured, if necessary at the cost of war. Official Germany, on the other hand, denied all territorial ambitions, and expressed its willingness to resign its right and interests and to recognize a French protectorate in return for reasonable compensation. Kiderlen-Wächter told Reventlow, himself a Pan-German, before the despatch of the Panther, that he did not wish for any territory in Morocco. He was also personally willing to cede Togoland in return for a large slice of the French Congo and the pre-emption of the Belgian Congo ; but the surrender of Togoland was disapproved and dropped. Rohrbach, the colonial specialist, has assured his fellow-countrymen since the outbreak of war that the Foreign Minister did not covet any part of Morocco, as his thoughts turned rather to ultimate acquisitions in the Belgian Congo and Angola. Bülow writes emphatically : " We never had any intention of taking possession of any part of Morocco." There is no trace of such a demand in the French Yellow Book or in the evidence of de Selves, the French Foreign Minister. If this description of the policy of the Kaiser, the Chancellor, and the Foreign Secretary is correct, the Mansion House threat appears needlessly provocative ; if it is false the warning becomes

* For a summary of the problem see the controversy between Mr. Morel and M. Philippe Millet in the Nineteenth Century, 1912. For fuller treatment see Morel, Morocco in Diplomacy ; Tardieu, ' Le Mystère d'Agadir ; ' ' Maurice,' ' La Politique Marocaine de l'Allemagne ' ; and Debidout, ' Histoire Diplomatique,' vol. ii., chapter 5.

fully intelligible. Sir Edward, it is obvious, was profoundly distrustful of the German Government in the opening weeks of the crisis ; and in his historic speech of November 27 he declared that it " had made demands with regard to the French Congo of an extent to which it was obvious that neither the French Government nor the French Chamber could agree." Here there is nothing about a demand for Moroccan territory. But the *Post* declared its disbelief in the Foreign Secretary's statement, and Tardieu attaches weight to the rumour that Kiderlen-Wächter had privately informed his political friends of his intention to take a part of the coast ; while Zimmermann, the Under-Secretary, is said to have told the President of the Pan-German League that the Government did not desire compensation in the Congo but a slice of Morocco. Amid this welter of suspicion and hypothesis there is at present no room for certainty.

The British threat created the same passionate resentment in Germany as the Tangier oration of 1905 had aroused in France and England. It was regarded as a wanton interference in a matter which concerned France and Germany alone, and as convincing evidence that Great Britain was as eager to thwart the colonial and commercial ambitions of Germany as she was to encourage those of France. For some weeks a European war seemed imminent. The Cabinet was divided on the question whether it should lend armed assistance to France ; but the signature of a treaty on November 4, ceding a slice of the French Congo and surrendering the right to the pre-emption of the Belgian Congo in return for the renunciation of German claims in Morocco, rendered an operative decision unnecessary. It was, however, widely known in Germany as well as in England that the fleet had been held ready for war ; and a statement by Capt. Faber, rebuked but not denied by the Foreign Secretary, that we had been fully prepared to enter the conflict was accepted as a new proof of our incurable hostility and our aggressive intentions. Only when the prolonged crisis was over did the nation learn the magnitude of the peril, and the Prime Minister sent Mr. Churchill to the Admiralty with orders to put the fleet into a condition of instant readiness for war.

The Morocco treaty was followed by the resignation of the indignant German Colonial Secretary, and was received with a howl of anger in chauvinist and Pan-German circles, which had expected a coaling-station at the very least, and which roughly criticized the Kaiser for his pusillanimity. The hostility to France was comparatively small, for she had been fighting for her own interests ; but throughout the autumn the nation seethed with indignation against England. The atmosphere was electric, and a spark might set it aflame.

X. From Agadir to Serajevo.

The Kaiser had stood out against the madness of his own warmongers, who were spoiling for a fight, and in the opening days of 1912 he asked that a member of the Cabinet should come to Berlin to discuss the situation. Both Sir Edward Grey and the Chancellor had publicly expressed a hope that now the Morocco question was out of the way, the relations of the two countries might improve. Lord Haldane was therefore deputed by the Cabinet to explain British policy to the German

Government.* On the first day of his visit he saw the
Chancellor, on the second the Kaiser and Tirpitz together,
and on the third the Chancellor again ; and in each case he
made it clear beyond the possibility of misunderstanding
that loyalty to the Entente with France and Russia was
and must remain the basis of British policy. The
discussions were frank and cordial ; but the old difficulties at once reappeared. The Chancellor renewed his
suggestion of a formula that neither country would enter
into any combinations against the other ; to which
Lord Haldane replied with the alternative proposal that
Great Britain should promise to take no part in an
unprovoked attack. He further asked what use it would
be to sign an agreement of amity if Germany simultaneously increased her fleet and Great Britain followed
suit. The reply once again was that a naval truce was
impossible without a political agreement. Temporary
retardation might be possible ; but such retardation,
though on a more generous scale than hitherto offered,
was to be an " understanding," not a written agreement.
Each party thus rejected the main proposal of the other ;
but the conversations were far from fruitless, and the
Tsar privately expressed his satisfaction at the success
of a visit in which each side convinced the other of its
sincerity and goodwill. Lord Haldane, however, was
most unfavourably impressed by the views and growing
influence of Tirpitz, whose programme of new construction, nevertheless, according to Reventlow, was
largely reduced in consequence of the visit of the British
statesman.

---

* In addition to the official declarations of the two Governments,
see Begbie, 'The Vindication of Great Britain,' chapter 3, and the third
edition of Reventlow's ' Deutschlands Auswärtige Politik.'

Lord Haldane reported the views of Berlin to his
colleagues, and a long discussion between the Chancelleries ensued, conducted, as Mr. Asquith informed
Parliament at the time, " in a spirit of perfect frankness
and friendship." The course of events has been described in the following memorandum issued by the
Foreign Office after the outbreak of war, which is so
important a statement of British policy that it must be
quoted in full.

" Early in 1912 the German Chancellor sketched to
Lord Haldane the following formula as one which would
meet the views of the Imperial Government :—

" 1. The high contracting parties assure each other
mutually of their desire of peace and friendship.

" 2. They will not either of them make or prepare to
make any (unprovoked) attack upon the other, or join in
any combination or design against each other for
purposes of aggression, or become party to any plan or
naval or military enterprise alone or in combination with
any other Power directed to such an end, and declare
not to be bound by any such engagement.

" 3. If either of the high contracting parties becomes
entangled in a war with one or more Powers in which it
cannot be said to be the aggressor, the other party will
at least observe towards the Power so entangled a
benevolent neutrality, and will use its utmost endeavour
for the localization of the conflict. If either of the high
contracting parties is forced to go to war by obvious
provocation from a third party, they bind themselves
to enter into an exchange of views concerning their
attitude in such a conflict.

" 4. The duty of neutrality which arises out of the
preceding article has no application in so far as it may

not be reconcilable with existing agreements which the high contracting parties have already made.

" 5. The making of new agreements which render it impossible for either of the parties to observe neutrality towards the other beyond what is provided by the preceding limitation is excluded in conformity with the provisions in article 2.

" 6. The high contracting parties declare that they will do all in their power to prevent differences and misunderstandings arising between either of them and other Powers.

" These conditions, although in appearance fair as between the parties, would have been grossly unfair and one-sided in their operation. Owing to the general position of the European Powers, and the treaty engagements by which they were bound, the result of Articles 4 and 5 would have been that, while Germany in the case of a European conflict would have remained free to support her friends, this country would have been forbidden to raise a finger in defence of hers.

" Germany could arrange without difficulty that the formal inception of hostilities should rest with Austria. If Austria and Russia were at war Germany would support Austria, as is evident from what occurred at the end of July, 1914 ; while as soon as Russia was attacked by two Powers France was bound to come to her assistance. In other words, the pledge of neutrality offered by Germany would have been absolutely valueless, because she could always plead the necessity of fulfilling her existing obligations under the Triple Alliance as an excuse for departing from neutrality. On the other hand, no such departure, however serious the provocation, would have been possible for this country, which was bound by no alliances, with the exception of those with Japan and Portugal, while the making of fresh alliances was prohibited by Article 5. In a word, as appeared still more evident later, there was to be a guarantee of absolute neutrality on one side, but not on the other.

" It was impossible for us to enter into a contract so obviously inequitable, and the formula was accordingly rejected by Sir E. Grey.

" Count Metternich upon this pressed for counter-proposals, which he stated would be without prejudice and not binding unless we were satisfied that our wishes were met on the naval question. On this understanding Sir Edward Grey, on the 14th March, 1912, gave Count Metternich the following draft formula, which had been approved by the Cabinet :—

" England will make no unprovoked attack upon Germany, and pursue no aggressive policy towards her.

" Aggression upon Germany is not the subject, and forms no part of any treaty, understanding, or combination to which England is now a party, nor will she become a party to anything that has such an object.

" Count Metternich thought this formula inadequate, and suggested two alternative additional clauses :—

" England will therefore observe at least a benevolent neutrality should war be forced upon Germany ; or

" England will therefore, as a matter of course, remain neutral if a war is forced upon Germany.

" This, he added, would not be binding unless our wishes were met with regard to the naval programme.

" Sir Edward Grey considered that the British proposals were sufficient. He explained that, if Germany desired to crush France, England might not be able to sit still, though, if France were aggressive or attacked Germany, no support would be given by His Majesty's Government or approved by England. It is obvious that the real object of the German proposal was to obtain the neutrality of England in all eventualities, since, should a war break out, Germany would certainly contend that it had been forced upon her, and would claim that England should remain neutral. An admirable example of this is the present war, in which, in spite of the facts, Germany contends that war has been forced upon her. Even the third member of the Triple Alliance, who had sources of information not open to us, did not share this view, but regarded it as an aggressive war.

" Sir Edward Grey eventually proposed the following formula :—

" The two Powers being mutually desirous of securing peace and friendship between them, England declares that she will neither make, nor join in, any unprovoked attack upon Germany. Aggression upon Germany is not the subject, and forms no part of any treaty, under-standing, or combination to which England is now a party, nor will she become a party to anything that has such an object.

" Sir Edward Grey, when he handed this formula to Count Metternich, said that the use of the word ' neutrality ' would convey the impression that more was meant than was warranted by the text ; he suggested that the substance of what was required would be obtained and more accurately expressed by the words ' will neither make, nor join in, any unprovoked attack.'

" Count Metternich thereupon received instructions to make it quite clear that the Chancellor could recom-

mend the Emperor to give up the essential parts of the
Novelle (the Bill then pending for the increase of the
German Navy) only if we could conclude an agreement
guaranteeing neutrality of a far-reaching character and
leaving no doubt as to any interpretation. He admitted
that the Chancellor's wish amounted to a guarantee of
absolute neutrality, failing which the Novelle must
proceed.

" Count Metternich stated that there was no chance
of the withdrawal of the Novelle, but said that it might
be modified ; it would be disappointing to the Chancellor
if we did not go beyond the formula we had suggested.

" Sir Edward Grey said that he could understand that
there would be disappointment if His Majesty's Government were to state that the carrying out of the Novelle
would put an end to the negotiations and form an
insurmountable obstacle to better relations. His Majesty's Government did not say this, and they hoped the
formula which they had suggested might be considered
in connexion with the discussion of territorial arrangements, even if it did not prove effective in preventing
the increase of naval expenditure.

" Sir Edward Grey added that if some arrangement
could be made between the two Governments it would
have a favourable though indirect effect upon naval
expenditure as time went on ; it would have, moreover,
a favourable and direct effect upon public opinion in
both countries.

" A few days afterwards Count Metternich communicated to Sir Edward Grey the substance of a letter
from the Chancellor in which the latter said that, as the
formula suggested by His Majesty's Government was
from the German point of view insufficient, and as His
Majesty's Government could not agree to the larger
formula for which he had asked, the Novelle must

proceed on the lines on which it had been presented to the Federal Council. The negotiations then came to an end, and with them the hope of a mutual reduction in the expenditure of the two countries."

When the third attempt to find a formula of reconciliation ended in failure, the situation might have seemed worse than ever ; but on neither side was the stock of goodwill exhausted. Germany's foremost diplomatist, Baron Marschall von Bieberstein, was brought from Constantinople to London. " I have long wanted to be ambassador to England," he remarked to his old friend Sir Edwin Pears, " because, as you know, I have for years considered it a misfortune to the world that our countries are not really in harmony. I consider that I am here as a man with a mission, my mission being to bring about a real understanding between the two nations." " Of his sincerity," adds Sir Edwin, " I have no doubt." His death from heart failure during the summer holidays was a tragedy. He was succeeded by a personal friend of the Kaiser, Prince Lichnowsky, whose unremitting efforts for reconciliation during the next two years are well known to his official and unofficial friends.

After the collapse of the negotiations initiated during Lord Haldane's visit, the Cabinet determined to define the exact character of the discussions between British and French experts which had been authorized in 1906. " We decided," declared Sir Edward Grey on August 3, 1914, " that we ought to have a definite understanding in writing, which was only to be in the form of an unofficial letter, that these conversations were not binding upon the freedom of either Government. On November 22, 1912, I wrote to the French Ambassador the following letter, and I received from him a letter in similar terms in reply :—

My dear Ambassador,—From time to time in recent years the French and British naval and military experts have consulted together. It has always been understood that such consultation does not restrict the freedom of either Government to decide at any future time whether or not to assist the other by armed force. We have agreed that consultation between experts is not, and ought not, to be regarded as an engagement that commits either Government to action in a contingency that has not yet arisen and may never arise. The disposition, for instance, of the French and British fleets respectively at the present moment is not based upon an engagement to co-operate in war.

You have, however, pointed out that, if either Government had grave reason to expect an unprovoked attack by a third Power, it might become essential to know whether it could in that event depend upon the armed assistance of the other.

I agree that, if either Government had grave reason to expect an unprovoked attack by a third Power, or something that threatened the general peace, it should immediately discuss with the other whether both Governments should act together to prevent aggression and to preserve peace, and, if so, what measures they would be prepared to take in common."

While these letters were being written the Balkan States had combined to expel Turkey from Macedonia and Thrace. The Great Powers, after vainly attempting to prevent the outbreak of the conflict, agreed to localize it ; but the Serbian invasion of Albania and her demand for an outlet on the Adriatic brought Russia and Austria to the brink of war. To deal with this and other problems Sir Edward Grey constituted an informal Areopagus of the ambassadors of the Great Powers in London under his chairmanship. Awkward corners, such as the delimitation of an independent Albania, were thus successfully turned, and his services to the peace of Europe were warmly acknowledged in Berlin and Vienna. " We have now seen," declared the German Foreign Secretary, Jagow, on February 7, 1913, " that we have not only points of contact with England of a sentimental nature, but that similar interests also exist. I am not a prophet ; but I entertain the hope that on the ground of common interests, which in politics is the most fertile ground, we can continue to work with England and perhaps to reap the fruits of our labours." Thus co-operation in practical work had at last appeared to accomplish what the search for abstract formulas failed to achieve. Taking advantage of the new born atmosphere of confidence and goodwill, the two Governments in the winter of 1913-14 proceeded to discuss two problems to which Germany attached the greatest importance. An adjustment of interests was at last reached in regard to the Bagdad railway, the joint exploitation of the petroleum springs in the Mosul vilayet, and the navigation of the Tigris. The future of the Portuguese colonies was again debated. Baron Beyens, who was Belgian Minister at Berlin at the time, states that Angola was earmarked as a German, and Mozambique as a British sphere of influence. Rohrbach declares that Germany was to have pre-emption whenever Portugal desired to sell Angola, contenting herself meanwhile with economic facilities. Whatever the exact details, an agreement highly gratifying to Germany was reached and initialled shortly before the outbreak of war. On this occasion at least there was no ground for the old complaint that Great Britain was a standing obstacle to the economic and colonial projects of the Fatherland. " We were frankly astonished by England's concessions," confesses Rohrbach, who finds in them evidence of her sincere desire for peace.* After such a testimony it is of little importance that the acid Revent-low discovers in the hesitation of Sir Edward Grey to publish the African treaty a proof of the bad faith which marked the whole transaction.† Well might Sir Edward Goschen, in his final interview with the Chancellor, speak of " the tragedy which saw the two nations fall apart just at the moment when the relations between them had been more friendly and cordial than they had been for years."

It is beyond the scope of this chapter to discuss the causes of the war or to describe the course of British policy in the fateful days preceding its outbreak. Alone of European statesmen the Foreign Secretary worked day and night for the preservation of peace ; but he was handicapped by the undefined character of our friendship with France. In his authoritative little book on ' The Foundations of British Policy,' written in 1911, the Editor of *The Westminster Gazette* declared that it was England's wish to combine friendships with independence, and that she had no desire to play a prominent part in Continental politics, as her main interests were elsewhere. Up to the very eve of war the Foreign Secretary and the Prime Minister repeatedly and categorically denied that the country had entered into pledges, written or unwritten, which would impede its freedom of action. And yet these assurances, however formally correct, were very far from being conclusive.

---

* See the article ' Wanted a Foreign Policy,' in The New Europe, Dec. 14, 1916.
† Deutschlands Auswärtige Politik, 3rd edition.

" We were tied to France inextricably," declares an
acute critic, " tied by countless invisible threads such as
fastened down Gulliver while he slumbered in the land
of little men."* " How far that friendship entails
obligation," declared Sir Edward himself on August 3,
1914, " let every man look into his own heart and his
own feelings and construe the extent of the obligation
for itself. I construe it myself as I feel it, but I do not
wish to urge upon any one else more than their feelings
dictate. The . House, individually and collectively,
may judge for itself." This was, indeed, so true that
when the Cabinet met to consider the crisis produced by
the ultimatum to Serbia, it was acutely divided, as in
1911, on the question whether in the event of war Great
Britain should intervene ; and the division lasted till
Germany decided the matter for the large majority by
her criminal violation of the neutrality of Belgium.

It is not necessarily a condemnation of the policy of
limited liability, though it suggests grave doubts as to
its wisdom, that every one was at liberty to " construe "
it for himself ; that the Cabinet was divided at a critical
moment ; that France counted on naval and military
aid as a debt of honour ; that Russia believed we should
be dragged in, and that Germany expected us to stand
out. Nor has the time yet come for a judicial verdict on
the whole policy of Continental commitments, unaccom-
panied as they were by an army of Continental dimensions
or by a frank explanation to Parliament and the nation
of their contingent liabilities. Looking back over the
crowded and anxious years, it is clear that on the one
hand it increased the probability of a war with Germany
by involving us in the quarrels and ambitions of our
friends, and that on the other it ensured that if a conflict
arose we should not be left to fight alone. The risk and

* *The Candid Review*, edited by Mr. Gibson Bowles, May, 1915.

the premium will have to be balanced against each other by the historical actuary of the future.   But whatever the judgment of posterity on its intrinsic merits or its technical skill, its foresight or its success, we may with some confidence anticipate a verdict that British policy throughout the period covered by this chapter was free from the slightest desire for territorial aggrandise- ment, and that the dearest wish of the British people was to maintain peace and promote goodwill among the nations of the earth.

G. P. GOOCH.

SHORT BIBLIOGRAPHY.

GENERAL.

The Annual Register; Debidour, 'Histoire Diplomatique de l'Europe, 1878-1916. 2 vols.

GREAT BRITAIN.

Lémonon, ' L'Europe et la Politique Britannique '; Gilbert Murray, ' The Foreign Policy of Sir Edward Grey '; Bertrand Russell, ' The Policy of the Entente: a Reply to Prof. Murray '; Sir E. T. Cook, ' How Britain strove for Peace '; Lord Esher, ' The Influence of Edward VII., and other Essays '; Begbie, ' The Vindication of Britain,' chap. 3.

JAPAN.

Sir R. Douglas, ' Europe and the Far East '; Hayashi, ' Memoirs.'

FRANCE.

Tardieu, ' France and the Alliances,' ' La Conférence d'Algésiras,' ' Le Mystère d'Agadir '; Barclay, ' Anglo-French Reminiscences '; Mévil, ' De la Paix de Francfort à la Conférence d'Algésiras '; Morel,' Morocco in Diplomacy '; Maurice, ' La Politique Marocaine de l'Allemagne.

GERMANY.

Prince Bülow, ' Imperial Germany ' (the editions of 1914 and 1916 should both be studied); Reventlow, ' Deutschlands Auswärtige Politik ' (the first and third editions should both be studied); Schiemann, ' Deutschland und die grosse Politik,' 1901-13 (annual volumes).

AUSTRIA.

Steed, ' The Hapsburg Monarchy,' chap. 4; Sosnosky, ' Die Balkan Politik Oesterreich-Ungarns,' vol. 2.

RUSSIA.

Trubetzkoi, ' Russland als Grossmacht '; Shuster, ' The Strangling of Persia '; Prof. Browne, ' The Persian Revolution.'